CHILDREN

with

HIGH-FUNCTIONING

AUTISM

CHILDREN
with
HIGH-FUNCTIONING
AUTISM
a parent's guide

Claire E. Hughes-Lynch, Ph.D.

PRUFROCK PRESS INC.
WACO, TEXAS

Library of Congress Cataloging-in-Publication Data

Hughes-Lynch, Claire E., 1967-
  Children with high-functioning autism : a parent's guide / Claire E. Hughes-Lynch.
    p. cm.
  Includes bibliographical references.
  ISBN-13: 978-1-59363-402-5 (pbk.)
  ISBN-10: 1-59363-402-1 (pbk.)
  1. Autism in children--Popular works. 2. Autistic children. I. Title.
  RJ506.A9H84 2010
  618.92'85882--dc22
                       2009053918

At the time of this book's publication, all facts and figures cited are the most current available. All telephone numbers, addresses, and website URLs are accurate and active. All publications, organizations, websites, and other resources exist as described in the book, and all have been verified. The author and Prufrock Press Inc. make no warranty or guarantee concerning the information and materials given out by organizations or content found at websites, and we are not responsible for any changes that occur after this book's publication. If you find an error, please contact Prufrock Press Inc.

Prufrock Press Inc.
P.O. Box 8813
Waco, TX 76714-8813
Phone: (800) 998-2208
Fax: (800) 240-0333
http://www.prufrock.com

Dedication

To Annalia and Nicholas

CONTENTS

Acknowledgements

I want to deeply thank my husband, James, who fed, cared for, and generally dealt with the mayhem while I was gone for 3 weeks at a time. I thank him for the years of working together and support for me, for us, and for our family since we've started down this road together. I love you, darling.

To my mother, Jami, who listened, read, bounced ideas, provided reiki and financial support at every step along the way, and who devised ways of dealing with an overactive, sleepless, anxious child without support, knowledge, or financial backing. She is the original mapmaker and someone I want to be just like when I grow up.

To our family, particularly Lia (Yiayia) who loved the sounds of her grandchildren, no matter how loud they yelled, and who prayed and played with the children; and to Papou Pete, Dampa, Maria, Haroula, Gran, and Grammy and their awareness of the power of love and genetics.

To my friends who listened, let me cry, and provided sustenance—both physical and emotional: Darla, Laura, and Linda; the Boyce, Johnson, Barker/Bergmann, Crespin, Kendall, and Hall families; Wendy, Elissa, Donna, Lou, Nicki, Christy, Tara, Cari, and Michelle—no matter where I am, there you are.

To the pets who provided therapy and unconditional love beyond what animals are supposed to do: Cody, Nellie, Chrissie, and even Bailey.

To the teachers who taught me about myself and my children, to look for strengths in the most challenging of behaviors and to think about other perspectives: Joyce, Elizabeth, Ginny, Lori, Kim, Amy, Nicki, Jane, Miss Gates, Mrs. Skaggs, and Mr. Kramer.

To our "angels" who loved and helped my children when I was too tired to keep going: Irene, Molly, Emmy, Amberly, Lori, and Zach—I am so grateful.

To Jay and Maureen McGowan for the McGowan Prize, which sent me to Oxford to study autism; and to the wonderful faculties at the College of Coastal Georgia, Bellarmine University, Florida Gulf Coast University, University of South Florida, Indiana University of Pennsylvania, The College of William and Mary, University of North Carolina at Greensboro, and the University of New Mexico. You rock!

To Webkinz, for providing entertainment that kept me going. This book would not have been finished if I hadn't toggled back and forth between Tile Towers and my manuscript.

To the publisher, Joel, and my editors, Jenny and Lacy, for their original idea and wanting to hear from both sides of me—the teacher of teachers and the parent.

To Rachel and Tina and the other mothers of children with autism whose stories, blogs, books, and support I depend on. Your work has led to many, many changes and so much awareness. I have such respect for you and your hard work blazing the trail.

And most importantly, to the biggest part of my heart, my children, whose stories I have shared and whose love I value every day. Mama's here. Mama's always here.

Introduction:
How Did I Get Here?

If you're not sure where you're going, you're liable to end up someplace else. If you don't know where you're going, the best made maps won't help you get there.

—Robert Mager, psychologist, writer, educator

AN UNPLANNED JOURNEY BETWEEN HOLLAND AND ITALY. SWITZERLAND?

It's important to know that no one chooses autism—you, your child, and your family were drafted. You need to remember this when teachers, other parents, and total strangers feel free to tell you that you're using autism as an excuse for _____ (name your issue here: misbehavior, laundry piling up, financial failure, your lack of showering . . .). Just like being drafted and being shipped off to another country, autism will change your whole life—your plans, your dreams, your family structure, and even your relationship with your local grocery store. Everything will be different than you expected, but not always in a bad way. Just . . . different.

This book was inspired by the essay "Welcome to Holland" by Emily Perl Kingsley (see Figure 1). I love this essay and present it to my college students when teaching Introduction to Disabilities, but I never really appreciated its wisdom until I sat crying as I reread it one night. I also realized that there was a lot of information about "Italy," or typical development, and "Holland," or children who had disabilities, but very little about children who were, well, different. Children who exhibited some, but not all of the characteristics; children who had some really significant strengths

Welcome to Holland
by Emily Perl Kingsley

I am often asked to describe the experience of raising a child with a disability—to try to help people who have not shared that unique experience to understand it, to imagine how it would feel. It's like this . . .

When you're going to have a baby, it's like planning a fabulous vacation trip—to Italy. You buy a bunch of guide books and make your wonderful plans. The Coliseum. The Michelangelo David. The gondolas in Venice. You may learn some handy phrases in Italian. It's all very exciting.

After months of eager anticipation, the day finally arrives. You pack your bags and off you go. Several hours later, the plane lands. The stewardess comes in and says, "Welcome to Holland."

"Holland?!?" you say. "What do you mean Holland?? I signed up for Italy! I'm supposed to be in Italy. All my life I've dreamed of going to Italy."

But there's been a change in the flight plan. They've landed in Holland and there you must stay.

The important thing is that they haven't taken you to a horrible, disgusting, filthy place, full of pestilence, famine and disease. It's just a different place.

So you must go out and buy new guide books. And you must learn a whole new language. And you will meet a whole new group of people you would never have met.

It's just a <u>different</u> place. It's slower-paced than Italy, less flashy than Italy. But after you've been there for a while and you catch your breath, you look around . . . and you begin to notice that Holland has windmills . . . and Holland has tulips. Holland even has Rembrandts.

But everyone you know is busy coming and going from Italy . . . and they're all bragging about what a wonderful time they had there. And for the rest of your life, you will say "Yes, that's where I was supposed to go. That's what I had planned."

And the pain of that will never, ever, ever, ever go away . . . because the loss of that dream is a very very significant loss.

But . . . if you spend your life mourning the fact that you didn't get to Italy, you may never be free to enjoy the very special, the very lovely things . . . about Holland.

Figure 1. Welcome to Holland essay.

that were both a result of and impacted by differences. There wasn't much information about children from "Switzerland" who aren't quite typical, but don't have classic disabilities—children like my child, who has high-functioning autism. And so, the idea for this book was created.

Throughout this book, the metaphor of traveling and maps will be used frequently. I found that there were lots of coping guides, lots of informative books, some "cures," and reams and reams of technical books. Most importantly, there were a small and growing number of first-person books written by families and individuals with autism. I am hoping that in this book you find a familiar voice of someone who refused to let autism win over her, her family, and her child; someone who refused to get overwhelmed, but found that there was hope, growth, and a really wonderful journey through it all. Switzerland, like Holland and Italy, has its own beauty!

MAPS AND AUTISM

"Welcome to Holland" originally was written for a child with intellectual disabilities (formerly referred to as mental retardation). However, it is an analogy to which I could deeply relate: You think you're going somewhere and suddenly you're not there. Autism is more like the *Wizard of Oz*: You think you're just like all of your friends and you think you're on the way with a clearly defined map, but then you start getting strange signs that things are not the same as all of the baby books would have you believe. I had read Vicki Iovine's *The Girlfriends' Guide to Pregnancy* and laughed so hard I was sobbing. (Seriously, my husband was concerned about me. Perhaps it was an overreaction to hormones. . . .) However, I truly bawled when I read the *The Girlfriends' Guide to Toddlers*. That wasn't what I was seeing. I didn't get to laugh at funny things my child was saying. I had the child who wouldn't leave the swings; I had the child who screamed at the idea of taking a bubble bath.

But I also had the child who could complete 100-piece puzzles at age 2; I had the child who at 10 months could understand when I told her that rocks broke apart to become sand and who could use that knowledge to bring herself back from the brink of overwhelming fear. I had the child who pulsed in his baby seat to the Muppets' song "Mahna Mahna" in perfect rhythm and banged on pots to Queen's "We Will Rock You" over and over again. Autism, yes, but gifts, nonetheless.

Autism is so insidious because, to use the Holland analogy, for a while, you *are* in Italy. The language spoken for a while is Italian. But in small pieces, the language changes. The people change. The activities change. The landscape changes. It reminded me for a while of one of those *Star Trek* shows where part of you was in one world and the other part was in another.

Yet, high-functioning autism isn't quite the Holland of "regular" autism. There are some real strengths, and there are traces of autism, but how much? There's a reluctance of professionals to diagnose anything. It's perhaps like being in Switzerland—a little bit of Italy, and closer to Holland than some of the other people in Italy, but not so close that you feel welcomed by the Dutch. Enough to see the abyss, but not to find the support. Switzerland can be very confusing.

There are several different metaphors about autism that people use. In her book *The Autism Trail Guide: Postcards From the Road Less Traveled*, Ellen Notbohm (2007) noted how having a child with autism is like being on a strange trip; you have to communicate with others that you've arrived safely and that you want to share your experiences. In contrast, Karyn Seroussi (2002) called autism "The Jabberwock" and talked about defeating the disease that causes autistic behaviors. She also talked about saving children from the "Pied Piper" of autism. It's interesting the different metaphors one finds—to some autism is a scary, demon thing; to others, it's a process and a journey.

That's autism: Something to be fought against while at the same time trying to understand the journey. It's both a process and a condition. It reminds me a bit of trying to capture the dual nature of light.

Scientists have found that when they provide a substance to react to, light clearly acts as a particle. When they provide a slit, it appears to be a wave. High-functioning autism is something our children have, as well as a characteristic of who they are. For me, living on the coast of Georgia, high-functioning autism is like the marsh, where the salt water and fresh water combine to form a vastly unique and fragile ecosystem. It's a really fine line between "quirky" and "problematic." A gap between "talented" and "not quite right." Somewhere between "cute" and "hmmmm."

MAPMAKER: WHO AM I TO WRITE THIS BOOK?

There are lots of books about autism out there: books written by people with doctorates and books written by mothers of children with autism, as well as numerous other books on the topic. This book happens to be written by a mother with a Ph.D. in special education and gifted education who has two children: one with high-functioning autism and another one with autistic-like behaviors. I'm writing this book because I read like a mad woman when I was going through my daughter's initial diagnosis and treatments. I was completely overwhelmed by information. There are so many sources of information available and so many view-points and so many arguments, I would turn off the computer in frustration after reading for hours, only to turn it on again the next morning to order the next book, to peruse another web page—trying to find someone or something to help. Some books really spoke to me; some books were a waste of my time. And some were, in my opinion, downright dangerous.

I am the mother of a daughter, "Elizabeth," who was identified with Pervasive Developmental Disorder, Not Otherwise Specified (PDD-NOS) at the age of 2 and identified as being gifted at the age of 7; and a son, "Raymond," who was diagnosed with Generalized Anxiety Disorder, Not Otherwise Specified (GAD-NOS) and Tourette's syndrome at age 6, and also identified as gifted at age 7. (For their own privacy, I have changed their names, as well as those of other children discussed in the book.) Because most of our lessons were learned through the experiences we had with our daughter, much of this book is based on our journey through the maze of her diagnosis, treatments, and future outlooks. However, where necessary, I also will focus on my son's issues. He is not diagnosed with autism, but has many similar issues. I've learned that this is not uncommon—siblings often will share characteristics, but have different labels.

However, in the irony of the universe, I received a doctorate in both special education and gifted education before I ever had children, and I am also a college professor in both of these areas. I "should" have been prepared for all of this, right? Wrong! I was familiar with the map of an educator, which is a vastly different map than that of a parent. This book is the middle ground of both parts of my life: my professional knowledge combined with, and at times, in conflict with, my personal role of "Mommy."

I have been taught through my training to focus on children's abilities. Twice-exceptional children, who are gifted with disabilities, are a particular passion of mine professionally. I have always loved working with children who have amazing insights and problem-solving abilities, but can't read for some reason. I loved the intellectual challenge of trying to figure out what would work with a twice-exceptional student—what reading strategy to use, what question to ask, and the like. What can I find to help *this* child develop his or her abilities, rather than be stymied by areas of challenge? But *this* child was now *my* child, and I had no professional knowledge of autism. I used to laugh ironically with my husband—give me a child who can reason but not read, and I'm all over that. But here, I have a child who can't talk! Talking is a strength of mine, to put it mildly. I drove my parents crazy talking; I got in trouble at school for talking. I went into a profession where I talk for a living! And *I* had a child who couldn't talk. Ah, the irony!

My own professional pride was a major "oughtism" that I encountered. I, of all people, with a Ph.D. in special education *ought* to know what to do. And I had not a clue. I now share a presentation with teachers called "The Other Side of the Table." I have been at countless Individualized Education Program (IEP) meetings as a teacher or advocate, translating terms and concepts and processes to parents. I have reassured them that I will do my best to help their child read, behave, make friends, and so on. I have always (after the first scary year of teaching) felt capable of doing so—knowing that there were lots of things to try and I would keep trying, and hopefully, something would work. But I also knew that children are so highly individual, that sometimes, nothing does. My job was not to give up on the family or the child, but to keep trying. I knew that as a teacher.

And then, I sat on the other side of the table, and I realized how little I knew about speech, autism, and Early Intervention processes—about anything—and how much I was depending on that person across from me to love my child, to help my child, and to know exactly what to do. I wanted her to tell me that she's seen lots of children like mine and all of them have been helped. I wanted her to see that yes, Elizabeth fixated on geography and could point to most of the states in the country, but this was not a problem, this was a strength. Perhaps Elizabeth would be a geographer one day and we could say, "It all started when she was 2." I needed that therapist to see her not as a problem to be solved, but a wonderful collection of abilities to be developed and grown. I needed her to know everything I didn't. I sat on that other side of the table and cried for someone to help my little girl, because I didn't know how.

I finally stopped crying when I read a marvelous book called *The Boy Who Loved Windows* by Patricia Stacey (2003). She is a phenomenal writer, and her story read like she was talking directly to me. She wrote of how her therapist said that one of the ways that parents of children with disabilities cope is by finding another child who had symptoms worse than their child's. Patricia was the "bottom" of the group—no child was worse off than hers. "My God!" I thought, "This works! Her child *is* worse off than mine!" But, you see, her child got better! By the end of the book, which I read in one long night, her son was talking and interacting and asking questions and learning—all of those things I worked on as a teacher developing talents. If *her* son could get better, maybe my daughter could too! Her book was the first hope I had that maybe we were on a path where Elizabeth could get better and be more of who she is—who she truly is. I had found my map.

SECOND THOUGHTS: HOW'D WE END UP HERE?

If you're reading this book, you're probably researching autism, trying to get a handle on this "thing," this "condition," this "disability." You've read countless books and web pages about autism that just don't quite paint the full picture of your child, and they don't quite capture that incredible ability that autism sometimes hides and sometimes makes more clear. You've read about autism and Asperger's syndrome, but still aren't sure what to tell your parents, your in-laws, or your child's teacher. You're almost certainly wondering what you can do and worrying about what you have done.

Second thoughts are like regrets: You can't have 'em because you can't fix 'em. You are making the best decisions you can right now with the information you have. Just like on any journey, you might wind up in a place that you're not really thrilled with. You might look at your house (a mess), your marriage (a mess), your relationships with others (a mess), and your child (oh, such a mess), and want to start over. You will probably obsess a bit: "If only I had . . ." The reality is that you did the best you could, and now you have to continue to do the best you can and get yourself through this mess, one piece at a time. Some advice my mother once gave me was, "You want this fixed *right now*, and it's just not going to happen. It will take time, and you have to give it that time."

No second thoughts also means that you don't give up, believing your-self to be a victim of circumstances, doctors, therapists, God, bad genes, or something else. As Rachel, a mother of a child with Asperger's, says,

> It can be extremely frustrating to deal with this disorder, but as much as a parent did not ask for a child with these issues . . . the child did not ask to be like this either. Ben describes his confusion as "birds in his head." We as parents need to take a step back, take a deep breath, and realize that the child is not intending to create chaos, he is just trying to cope with it. The more we understand this disorder and let the child know that we understand how he is feeling, the better off he will be.

As in any trip, you are certainly allowed to cry when you wonder, "How on Earth did I get here?" Now it is time to go and build yourself a map to get through it.

WHY DO WE HAVE TO GO?

The causes of autism are fiercely debated. What we do know is that the rate of identified autism, all categories, has dramatically increased around the world in the last 20 years. There is a wonderful commercial, put out by the organization Autism Speaks and the Ad Council, which shows a cute little girl in a dance outfit. It states, "Chances of being in a Broadway show? 1:11,000. Chances of a child being diagnosed with autism? 1:150. It's time to listen."

It may be even more prevalent than that. Recent surveys, led by teams with Dr. Kogan from the Health Resources and Services Administration and Dr. Blumberg from the Centers for Disease Control and Prevention (CDC; 2009), found that 1 in 91 children have a diagnosis of autism spec-trum disorders (ASDs), and because it is more commonly diagnosed in males, 1 in 58 boys do. In December of 2009, the CDC released a report that cited prevalence rates of 1 in 110 children in the United States having a diagnosis of autism spectrum disorders. Up until 1990, there were very few children diagnosed with any form of autism; it was considered a low-incidence disorder and only children who had extreme cases were diagnosed.

So, what happened in 1990?

It is true that along with autism, the rates of other disorders have increased as well, although not to the same degree as autism. According to Jun Yan (2008), using information from the Centers for Disease Control and Prevention, diagnoses of Attention Deficit/Hyperactivity Disorder (ADHD) also have dramatically surged. Between 1980 and 1990, the rates of learning disabilities (LD) dramatically increased. According to Drs. Wright and Cummings (2005), there has been a shift in the diagnosis paradigm from evaluating people as "normal" or "abnormal" to evaluating their symptoms as "problematic" or a "disease" to be treated. In other words, it is very natural for a person going through a divorce to be depressed and not function well at work. This is "normal." However, is depression and inability to work a problem? Yes, and therapists are much more likely to encourage someone to seek counseling and to prescribe medication now then they were 30 years ago.

Even the concept of what is a problem has changed in our society. Matthew Smith, in a 2009 paper presented at the Congress of the Humanities and Social Sciences, noted that ADHD is a relatively new construct. In the 1950s, schools were pressured to produce students who could compete on an international level. The demands for children to sit and learn passively became an issue for children with more active learning styles and the rates of ADHD and learning disabilities skyrocketed.

Similarly, autism, meaning "state of being within oneself," wasn't even named until 1943, when Leo Kanner wrote a paper describing children who were very withdrawn and exhibited odd behaviors and language problems. In 1944, Hans Asperger also noted this, but his children did not have language delays, thus leading to the differences between children identified with Asperger's syndrome and those with autism. Although autism certainly has existed under other names (including insanity or mental retardation), many of the children on the spectrum now would not have been diagnosed with anything until recently. They were just considered "quirky." Did they experience emotional and learning problems as a result of their quirkiness? Of course, but that wasn't perceived as enough of a reason to treat them professionally. Too often, parents and schools were perceived as the source of any problems, and therefore as the source of any solutions.

Now, insurance companies regularly cover mental as well as physical health as an awareness of our ability to work on problems, even if they're normal ones, increases. Similarly, people are more willing to seek help for things that are considered problems now, when they would have been told to "buck up" 40 years ago. That guy in my mom's high school class who thought he was from Venus? Probably Asperger's. My husband who clears his throat frequently and has digestive issues when he's stressed out? Probably Tourette's syndrome. My tendency to procrastinate until the very last possible moment on an important task? Probably anxiety disorder. But such labels weren't widely used 40 years ago (although there has been a gradual acceptance of them over time).

And with such a shift to diagnosing problems rather than disease, a more relaxed definition came into being. The numbers shift constantly; it is hard to get a handle on what criteria are being used. Are we diagnosing classic autism, or the full spectrum? Are we diagnosing more because the criteria have changed to include children who would have been excluded before?

Regardless of the shifting numbers, autism is being diagnosed at skyrocketing rates that appear to have only a little to do with our society's acceptance of labels and willingness to provide therapy for problems. A survey of autism labels in California schools by the organization Fighting Autism (n.d.) found that autism diagnoses had increased more than 1,100% over the last 10 years. In addition, according to Dr. Karp

(2009) of the University of California, Los Angeles, it's being diagnosed around the world in increasing rates. In other words, autism is being diagnosed now in England, Spain, Holland, and even Pakistan, in similar rates to the United States when using the entire spectrum rather than the more limited classic autism diagnosis (Maqbool, 2009). Epidemic? Perhaps . . . but certainly a real problem. It did explain to me why it was so hard to tell people from other generations; why the word "autism" was whispered by my mother-in-law, why my children's teachers flinched when I said that Elizabeth had autism. Expectations about autism in people of other generations or who had educational training more than 10 years ago are very different than the perceptions parents and new educators have today.

Personally, all I cared about was that I had a child who was not speaking and who seemed to be struggling in her daily experiences; a child to whom sand sliced and hurt; a child with strong abilities I wanted to see developed and not neglected. A friend of mine has a son who could only relate to people by comparing them to colors. Another friend has a son who does not sleep. They are all exhausted beyond belief and she and her husband are divorcing. The skyrocketing numbers of diagnoses do mean that there is more research, more funds, more insurance, more help. And more help is what is needed. I'm in favor of anything that provides help!

But what *causes* it? Regardless if there's a problem—why?

CAUSES—A FOGGY PATH

All symptoms have to have a cause. For a while I didn't care *why* Elizabeth had autism, just that she had it, and I wanted to know what could be done to help her. After a while, I realized that one's belief in the cause of autism impacts the choice of treatments. What I could *do* was directly related to *why*. I had to make sense of my beliefs of why in order to help her.

Refrigerator Mothers

I have to include this as a perception, *not* a cause, related to autism. In 1943, Leo Kanner, one of the first authorities on autism, noticed that there was a marked lack of affection between mothers and children diagnosed with autism. Furthered by Bruno Bettleheim in 1962, the theory placed the blame almost solely on the environment of parenting. You can hear traces of it in an older generation who urges you to just "love it out of 'em," or conversely blames you by saying something like, "If you were a better mother. . . ." And we hear it in ourselves as we question our own parenting abilities.

Clearly, Kanner and Bettleheim (a) did not notice that these same mothers often had very loving relationships with their other children, and (b) were blaming the lack of closeness on the mother, not the inherent lack of response on the child. Rachel, a friend of mine, tells the story of the first time her son hugged her—at age 4!

> I was dropping him off at preschool and gave the regular wave goodbye after an encouraging pat on the back and a wishing of a good day. As I was leaving the room, he stood up and said, "Wait Mom." I stopped in my tracks, turned around, and saw him coming toward me with the most sincere face I had ever seen him have. He gave me a little hug. I hugged him back and told him I loved him. Then as he went back to his seat, I found myself in a daze, that had never happened before . . . ever.
>
> As a baby, Ben had colic and acid reflux. There were many days where I would go back to bed at night in the same clothes I had on the day before. The first 3 months were spent trying to comfort him and then just letting him cry himself to sleep in his room, with the door shut, because I had had all I could take. He would scream and cry for hours, and as hard as that is to believe, it would be literally for hours. I had a very hard time bonding with him as a baby and don't think I actually did. A lot of guilt

came with that, and I would always blame myself when he did not look at me or respond to me with a connection that I had seen with other mothers. He would hang off of me when I carried him and it seemed that I was just there to provide his needs. When you have tried hugging your child, only to have him stand there and not really hug back, it is hard. So when he finally initiates a hug, it is as if the sky opened and clarity rained down upon you . . . the realization that you are doing something right.

Dr. Bernard Rimland, in his 1964 book *Infantile Autism*, was the first authoritative voice to debunk Kanner and Bettelheim's views that the parental bond was the environmental factor and to propose that autism has a neurological and physiological cause. But the damage was done, and we have spent decades since trying to persuade others that our children are loved and not "spoiled."

Genetics

Studies have found links to autism on 21 of the 23 chromosomes, with a great deal of emphasis being paid to the X chromosome in particular (Simons Foundation for Autism Research, 2009). Certainly, autism appears to run in families. We personally have traced many of my daughter's issues back to specific family members. However, it's not a clear-cut connection. It appears to be a series of "switches" at the genetic level that have to be "turned on." In other words, it appears that children might be created at conception with the *potential* for autism, which then is triggered by something in the environment, or a particular combination of genetic issues that together create autism—both during gestation and afterward. Merely having one genetic marker is not enough—they have to occur together in a particular sequence and interact with each other. Certainly, weeks 8–24 are the time of developing neurological growth during pregnancy, and trauma during this time could affect the brain without causing physical disabilities.

This is a belief that I hold. I certainly can see some of the tendencies of autism in both my family and that of my husband. I know that our family dynamics often are based around these tendencies, and we have come up with interesting coping strategies. For example, my uncle has always hated being touched. My great-aunts, grandmother, and mother recoil when they are touched on the face. Our favorite ice cream is any kind with nuts because of its texture. We laugh in our family about how we deal with our aversions to things; we use "close, but not touching" to indicate affection; we make sure to have textured foods available; air conditioning is adjusted away from the face; and emotional things are dealt with lightly. My husband's family is similar—emotional issues are dealt with in small doses; the house has to be arranged perfectly before one leaves; top sheets are left off because they are too "tickle-y;" and stressful situations are to be avoided at all costs. The keys for my being able to work with Elizabeth lived within the strategies our families had taught us, and perhaps other strategies out there. I have since become fascinated with strategies intervention because of my belief that her autism lives in our genes.

Mirror Neurons

There is a link between the lack of mirror neurons in people and autism, according to Dr. Oberman (2005) and other researchers at the University of California, San Diego. Mirror neurons are neurons that turn on both when you do something and when you observe someone else doing the same thing. If you see a sad movie and cry, your neurological system is taking the information you've observed and turning on the same neurons that you turn on yourself when you're truly sad. In other words, you can cry at *Beaches* and you don't have to have your best friend actually die in order to feel distraught. Similarly, you can feel joy watching the winner from *American Idol* perform or anger reading about torture. It doesn't have to happen to you directly to feel it.

People with autism have a dysfunctional mirror neuron system, which means that they don't feel the emotions that other people around them are feeling, or have the same awareness of other people's emotions or feelings. In fact, although they may be aware of their own emotions, they might believe that others share their viewpoint. These mirror neurons are responsible for empathy with others, and lack of empathy or even awareness of others can lead to significant social challenges. This dysfunction of the neural development can account for much of the self-absorption that children with autism exhibit.

Mercury Link/Immunizations

Children with autism act almost exactly like people who we know have been exposed to mercury. When neurons and nerves are exposed to mercury, they shrink and fairly dramatically die. Fierce arguments have grown up concerning the impact of mercury in immunizations and numerous conspiracy theories abound about the government's role in promoting immunizations over the health of its children.

Certainly there could be better immunizations. Children today receive enormous times the number of immunizations that children born in the 1960s received. In 2006, Jenny McCarthy called for the Centers for Disease Control and Prevention to "get the crap out" of immunizations. The list of heavy metals in immunizations is stunning. Certainly, it could do no harm to clear out the elements that are potentially harmful. Additionally, it could do no harm to look at the immunization schedule. Do we *really* have to bombard our littlest people with megadoses of immunizations before they've fully developed their own immune systems? Isn't it possible to spread out the immunizations and break them into smaller doses?

Plus, and this is big, folks, there are a lot more things that could more likely cause autism that we are *not* getting upset about. Mercury in the soil and the air? Mercury in your fillings? Hormones in your water? Phthalates in your plastics? Don't hear much about those things on the 6 o'clock news.

What is on the news are the court cases by parents who are suing the government, claiming that the Measles-Mumps-Rubella (MMR) shot caused their child's autism. Every single one of the court cases that claim autism occurred due to vaccination has been denied. However, and it is worthwhile noting, many court cases that have claimed *physical* damage from the overload of immunizations have won. Cases such as *Banks v. Secretary of the Department of Health and Human Services* (decided in 1994) have found that the MMR shot led to acute disseminated encephalomyelitis of the brain. The court said in its decision that Bailey Banks' brain condition quite possibly led to behavioral changes, because he "more likely than not suffers from PDD, and not from autism" (p. 14)—a very fine discrimination, David Gorski (2009) noted, as Pervasive Developmental Disorder-Not Otherwise Specified (PDD-NOS) is on the autism spectrum, while Pervasive Developmental Delay (PDD) is not. Thus, *all* court cases claiming an immunization-autism link have failed, but many that have claimed compensation for intervening physical diseases have succeeded.

But my belief is that immunizations are not necessarily the issue—our global living is—a belief that is shared and being studied now by the federally funded National Children's Study (2009). The amount of hormones and various drugs in our water and our meat is staggering. The ubiquitous plastic containers that we store our food in and drink from have harmful substances. There are skyrocketing rates of mercury around the world in our soil, our oceans, and our air. The amount of just mercury in our ecosystem has gone off the charts. A 1995 study by William Fitzgerald of the University of Connecticut found that in the 100 years prior to the study, the amount of mercury in the air increased 300%, with most of the increase occurring since 1970. Emissions have dramatically increased in the United States since governmental oversights were removed. Other countries, such as India and China have almost no governmental oversight. Certainly we see problems with mercury in the tuna pregnant women are not supposed to eat, the shrimp we're all supposed to eat in moderation, and the smog over our cities. Heck, mercury was in our tooth fillings until recently. The reality is that mercury is in everything—if it's in the soil, the water, and the air, there's nothing we eat, nothing we drink, and nothing we wear that has never encountered mercury. Immunizations are certainly problematic, but there are much bigger problems with mercury and other environmental toxins than the trace amounts found in the MMR shot. Our very ecosystem is threatening us.

Food Allergies

With the issues of headaches, skin problems, digestion, diarrhea, and general bowel disturbances that many children on the spectrum have, there is some evidence to indicate that some children are born with intestinal allergic reactions to irritants, particularly dairy, wheat, and for some children, corn. Certainly the use of corn syrup, gluten, and milk are much higher in our foods today than they were just 50 years ago. In her 2002 book, Karyn Seroussi wondered if such allergic reactions and the consequential autistic behaviors mimic typical people's reactions to hallucinogenic drugs, such as LSD or "magic mushrooms." Many other parents have noted that their children have inordinately high levels of yeast in their urine and stool samples. Many researchers, including Drs. Bernard Rimland, William Shaw, and others, have been investigating this linkage between diet and autism for some years now, but the mainline perspective is that it is unproven (see Rimland, Crook, & Crook, 2001; and Shaw et al., 1998).

Certainly, in our family, we are known for lactose intolerance. I personally was given goat's milk rather than cow's milk as a child because of my mother's observation of my sleeplessness and erratic behaviors when I drank cow's milk. My friend Tina's son tested as being not lactose intolerant, but she noticed significant behavioral changes when he had milk. My husband and daughter both have the flushed cheeks and dark circles under their eyes that often are symptoms of allergies. My husband and I have noticed that we go through phases of "milk addiction" when we're anxious because of the feeling of relaxation and calm we get from drinking milk. One of the most frustrating things about allergies is that children (and adults) often crave the very thing that they're allergic to. Many, many families of children with autism have noticed that before they cut off dairy products, their children craved milk and that milk or bread would be the only thing that could calm them down. Some researchers, such as Auld and Grootendorst (2004), have found that milk is more addictive than alcohol and cigarettes. Certainly, diet can impact behavior.

It should be noted that some doctors view allergies only as a reaction identifiable with a skin test. Reactions to food may not show up in a skin test, and they may use the term intolerances as opposed to allergies.

A friend of mine once referred to children with autism as the "canaries in our world." Living in Kentucky as we did for a while, mining references are common. In the days before monitors, miners would send down a canary into the mine before the first run to test the air that had been shut up all night. If the canary came back alive, the air was good; if the canary came back dead, the air was bad and they would have to take measures to make the mine safe again. The sheer numbers of children being diagnosed with autism are telling us something. What that something is, though, is hotly debated.

I refuse to become a victim, but I get so incredibly angry when I think that our own world might have poisoned my children.

Starting the Journey: From the Beginning—and Even Before

1

On March 6, 2001, our family began. Our daughter, Elizabeth was born at 5:25 in the afternoon after 12 hours of labor. She was a much-wanted child that we had been trying to conceive for more than a year. Because of fibroids and other issues, it had been hard to get her. I remember crying, realizing that it seems so easy to conceive in your teens and twenties, but here I was in my 30s and with caution thrown to the wind, all of those years of desperately trying *not* to get pregnant were coming back to haunt me. We cried and celebrated that day in July when the stick showed two lines of pink.

BRAIN DEVELOPMENT ISSUES

Often mothers of children with autism will report that they had a feeling of something "not quite right" even while they were pregnant. There are some genetic studies, according to Michael Szpir (2006), that seem to indicate that the genetic alterations that can turn into the propensity for autism occur around 8 weeks after conception. Sometimes not, but there often is the mother's instinct that something's off. I *loved* being pregnant, and I was always aware of another life force within me. I truly believed in God after being pregnant because of that connection to *life* and a sense of growing. However, 12 weeks into my pregnancy, we had a scare when an ultrasound found a fiber wrapped around her little tiny fetus head. Often found around arms and legs, these fibers could stunt the growth of the limb. We knew that there was no way the baby could survive with the fiber wrapped around her head. Our obstetrician took a wait-and-see attitude, and many prayers later, no sign of the fiber was present at 16 weeks. But there were fibroid tumors in my uterus that were *huge* and growing and the poor baby was curled around them. Throughout my whole pregnancy we were holding our breath. However, my water broke when she was 37 weeks and she was delivered vaginally and relatively stress-free—a healthy, 6 pound, 12 ounce little girl. The challenge of the pregnancy made me so relieved that she was "normal" at birth that I never questioned some of her odd antics as a baby. She was pink and beautiful and all potential.

Her birth story is different than many children with autism because it was the pregnancy that was stressful, not the actual birth. Ray's birth is more typical of a birth reported by mothers of children with autism. His labor was about an hour from 0–10 dilation, with only 2 hours of active contractions. In the birth process, the muscles of the birth canal contracted so fiercely, he was born with a significant cephalohematoma or cone. Lots of babies are born cone-headed, but the lump on ours was almost as big as the rest of his head. It was quite disturbing. The doctors told us to watch the lump and that it could take up to a year to go down.

There was a good deal of "Well, we'll have to wait and see. It should be fine," which was just vague enough to worry us. To our great relief, it had rounded off after about 4 months, but the pressure of those contractions pushed significantly on his brain.

Both children also were quite jaundiced and did not receive treatment in a timely manner. They released us from the hospital one day after birth, and we were told that they might be a little jaundiced and to put them in the sun. Not a real problem finding sun in Southwestern Florida! So, we bathed our little darlings in sunshine until their first appointments at one week. In both cases, the pediatrician found significantly elevated jaundice levels that were "coming down," indicating higher levels before that would have required the bili lights. Even in the case of my son, where we were looking for problems, we were told "You're fine" by the hospital and told later by our pediatrician that we had gone into the danger zone of bilirubin. Jaundice can carry the possibility of brain damage. Not often, but it can.

Ray also had a terrible fall onto a concrete floor where he hit the front of his head when he was 7 months old. He did not pass out, and the x-ray came back OK, but again I heard the cheery doctor voice of "He should be fine. Just wait and see."

Do we have MRI data that our children have brain trauma? No. But there is the underlying fear and niggling concern of what happened and "if only . . ." thinking. I still sense that some of their issues were triggered by some form of brain pressure or injury—both in utero and afterward. In addition, there is a common theme of head trauma or high fevers noted among mothers of children with autism.

Rachel's Story

My pregnancy with Ben was as normal as could be. Blood pressure, weight gain, growth rate: all good. Then came delivery day. After 10 hours of unmedicated intense labor, I finally resolved that this was not going to happen without medication. I took the epidural and things calmed down, at least until it came time to push. I was ready to go and so was Ben. After just a few times, the nurse's face turned to grave concern, and she told me to stop immediately. Was I doing it wrong? Apparently my tailbone was digging into his forehead each time I pushed and his heartrate kept dropping in half. An emergency C-section had to be done and the nurse had to then push him back up through the birth canal. We have heard from other parents that they too experienced a traumatic birth and that frontal lobe trauma is a common factor.

Ben also had to have surgery to correct a hydra seal in his scrotum when he was 4 months old. He was taken back to surgery with a smile on his face and woke up a few hours later a different baby. We were told that he would not even remember the surgery and be back to the happy baby we had in no time. It was a few weeks before we started thinking that something had gone wrong during the surgery because our happy baby was not back. He seemed more introverted and irritated. Neither of us had experience in raising babies, so we just kept trying our best to do the right thing. We later heard from a psychologist that it is unusual that we were not permitted to be with him while he was undergoing anesthesia, and I regret that I couldn't be with him during the surgery to protect him. We will never know if something did go wrong.

HINDSIGHT IS 20/20: ISN'T THAT CUTE? . . . BUT SOMETHING'S NOT QUITE RIGHT

Autism is sneaky. I can look back now and say, "Ahhhh, so that was the autism coming out." But at the time. . . . I have backgrounds in both gifted education and special education, and my gifted education experience means I tend to look at kids from a strengths-based perspective. I see things that could be the germ of a talent or activities that show promise of great thinking. Even with a special education background, I tend not to look at things from a deficit view. One of the most significant challenges of working with two different sets of professionals is that one might see a behavior as characteristic of a deficit, while the other sees the behavior as evidence of a strength.

For example, as an infant, Elizabeth would get the cutest expression on her face when she was startled. Her eyes would get round, her mouth would open, and arms would fly out at the slightest change in her environment. We were intrigued at this and said, "Wow! What an alert child we have!" and I would spend some time soothing her. It's a startle reflex that infants have and adults still have to some degree. It's more than surprise—it's an instinct that infants use to let themselves know that something has changed, and it activates their "fight or flight" adrenaline rush. Heart rates accelerate, pupils dilate, and the body tenses up, ready for action. All infants have it, but infants who later develop autism often have a very sensitive startle reaction. In other words, they don't normalize very quickly—the world is a very nerve-wracking place that causes high anxiety.

Another example: When she was 9 months old, my daughter would bang on the dryer and then listen to the differences as she banged on the washing machine. Then, she would repeat her actions. Repeat. Repeat. For about 30 minutes. Isn't that cute? We were convinced she would either be a drummer or a repairwoman. She spent an hour at a time listening to the different sounds of the bangs. She still has this skill of distinguishing little details and analyzing how things are alike and different. Hidden Picture games are no fun for her because she just points right at the missing objects. I had to explain to her once that this is hard for most of us, and it's fun for us because it's a challenge. She just shrugged. Now, of course, I know that it's the autism combined with an eye for detail, but at the time, we were very impressed with her ability to concentrate and discriminate.

As a baby, Elizabeth insisted very definitely on being held facing outward. She would cry and strain her head around trying to see around me when I held her facing me. So, I happily turned her around so that her back was to me and she was free to observe the world around her. I was pleased to have such a curious and exploratory child. Because of an old back injury, I couldn't carry her in one of those front sling-style packs, so I ended up with the baby on my hip, watching the world from a slightly tipped angle at times. However, putting her down was a real challenge.

Elizabeth *hated* tummy time—not just resisted it, but *hated* it. I was a good mommy of the early 2000s who laid her child down on her back to avoid Sudden Infant Death Syndrome (SIDS). We were deeply grateful that we lived in Florida so that the whole issue of blankets was not a concern. She would go into her little onesies, lie down on the big crib mattress, and play contentedly, often soothed by the mobile. But get her up and put her down on the floor face down and she would turn into this monster of a child who would shriek uncontrollably for hours. I at first thought that she would cry herself to sleep, but no such luck. For the first 5 months of her life, Elizabeth experienced this Jekyll-and-Hyde transformation every time we turned her over onto her stomach. Tummy Time became Torture Time—for everyone. I tried the nifty mat with the colors and activities. I tried no mat. I tried a soft texture. I tried the cold tile floor. In all cases, we had unrelenting crying.

Once she learned to roll herself over, around 5 months old, we would put her on her little mat and she would immediately roll herself over onto her back to play with her toes. All of the baby books said not to worry about this—that the baby's head will round out when she can hold her head up. But our baby spent so much time on her back looking out at the world that her actual head shape was altered. Needless to say, Elizabeth is now 8 years old and still has a flat spot on the back of her head. When I'm rubbing her head, I am always reminded of the Western Native American babies who were carried on flat boards, or "papoose boards," and had flat heads. Flat heads used to be a significant cultural trait encouraged among some Native American populations in the West, and the White men and other tribes were called "round heads" when the cultures collided. There's even a Flathead Reservation and a Flathead River in Montana named after this practice. However, I know that for us, her flat head is a symptom and symbol of her autism—hidden, but still faintly perceptible.

Rachel's Story

Even at an early age, Ben was driven by color. He had to have a specific colored cup, plate, utensils . . . everything. He arranged his cars in order of color and the most significant recollection of his need to organize by color was an activity cube that had colored pegs and slots to put them in. He was only 6 or 7 months old when we found the cube with all of the pegs arranged in the slots by color. It was actually our first realization that this child was a bit different.

Around the age of 2 he began to assign colors to family and friends. Based on your relationship to him, you were assigned a color. Mom = yellow, Dad = blue, brother Charlie = green, both grandfathers were red, and ironically his one grandfather's girlfriend was assigned orange, which is the combination of authoritative yellow (Mom) and fun red (grandfathers). The same was applied to his fun aunt.

Once he began understanding family relationships, he no longer used colors to comprehend the relationship of a person to himself, but during that time it was fun to see what colors he would assign people. At the time we just thought it was just another quirky thing that he did.

There comes a time when you begin to realize that something really isn't normal or even "cute" anymore.

I remember Elizabeth playing in the bathtub, happy and content as she watched the water run through her fingers. She was sitting in one of those bath seats that kept her sitting up while I could wash her and her hair. She loved bath time, until the washing part. She would submit to my washing her hair, which she didn't like, but didn't stress out about too much. Then, the water would rinse off the soap and she would go ballistic. I remember being very proud of myself when I finally realized that she was afraid of the rainbows of the soap bubbles reflecting on the surface of the water. She was 9 months old and scared of rainbows in the water.

Hair washing and haircuts are frequent issues among children with autism. My friend Tina would cut her son's hair while he slept over the course of several days. "Badly," she emphasized, "but at least he didn't have hair in his eyes anymore." We were determined that we would win the haircut battle with my son, and it took three adults to hold him down in the stylist's chair one memorable day when he was 2. I was determined that he would *not* win this battle, but afterward, when we had tipped the stylist more than the haircut itself cost, I realized that this was something we would have to grow into.

There were other sensory issues that posed concerns. We lived in Florida about a mile and a half from the beach. We never went. From the time of her birth until she was about 2 years old, Elizabeth *hated* the sand. She liked the water all right, until a wave would hit her in the face. But the sand . . . she would try to climb my legs to get away from it. Later, I tell the story of how she overcame her fear of sand, but only after we worked on overcoming that fear for more than a year.

Babies with autism will often lock into sensory stimuli that scare or intrigue them. In our case, I realized after the fact that her love of different sounds, fear of water reflections, her hatred of tummy time, and her abhorrence of sand were part of the sensory seeking and avoidance facets of autism. That sensory input was too much for her to handle. And such sensitivities are highly individual to each child. I have a friend whose son hates green—but only a particular shade of it. Dark green—fine. But light, bright green—no go. One memorable dinner at our house a plate of peas was presented to him (along with a hamburger and French fries—I *was* trying to be a good hostess!), resulting in the beginning of a meltdown, whereupon my friend and the child had to leave immediately. Such immediate leavings often are a symptom of the recognition that you don't get to live the same life that other mothers seem to get to live.

Similarly, babies with autism often hate being touched. When Elizabeth was an infant, I bought a book about baby massage—how it's so good for developing nervous systems, how it can calm them down, how it's a wonderful soothing process right before bed. Not for us. Elizabeth loved to be held, but not rubbed in any way. She turned over for the first time as I was trying to calm her down by rubbing her back—she squirmed so much away from it, she flipped herself over. She was so surprised, but soon mastered the art of flipping! Many, many mothers tell about how their child hated, or passively withstood, being hugged, touched, or otherwise shown affection. In her 2003 book, *The Boy Who Loved Windows*, Patricia Stacey noted that it isn't because they have no feelings, but that they are so completely overwhelmed by their feelings of neediness and love that they avoid the situation that causes such intense emotions. Thus, hugging and loving has to be carefully controlled so that they aren't overwhelmed by the intensity of their emotions.

You quickly learn as a parent to avoid certain situations, certain textures, or certain places. You accept things that you never imagined you would find acceptable. It's frustrating when you realize that your child's issues are controlling your life—and everyone else has something to say about that.

WARNING SIGNS: DOCTORS, MOTHERS-IN-LAW, AND THE PUBLIC

Three little words can trigger you to know that *something* is wrong beyond your child being quirky. You will hear them time and again from your mother, your mother-in-law, from complete strangers at the grocery store—even you will say them once in a while. These three words will be directed either at you or your child and you will soon learn to wince— hard—at them: "Can't you just . . ."

Behave? Say "hello" to our neighbor? Play nicely with the children on the play date? Stop buzzing? Go to sleep? Wear the nice pretty dress for Easter? Make him stop? Tell her to be quiet? Get her off the swings? Clean up those crushed Cheerios?

These words will haunt you at home until you can educate everyone who comes into your house. They will be everywhere in public. My reactions ranged from shrieking back at the judgmental idiot, to apologies, to stone cold silence. I still remember one airline flight attendant who had *not* helped *at all* during a long early morning flight from Boston to Florida while both of my children were fussing and wailing and trying to make everyone else around us miserable as well. I finally appeased them somewhat by opening a box of Cheerios. An hour later, there were Cheerios smashed into the corners of the seat, ground in the children's hair, and in dust on the floor. Yes, we left a mess. But I figured that it wasn't anything a vacuum couldn't take care of, and much better than the alternative of screaming toddlers for 2 ½ hours. I truly was sorry—and no, I couldn't "just" get them to stop. And did I mention that the flight attendant *never* offered to help? No offers to hold a child, no in-your-face-peek-a-boo, nothing—other than a lecture about how she could not believe the mess we had left and did we not realize how rude that was? Well, yes, I did—but I figured that it was better than top-of-the lungs caterwauling of *two* toddlers at 6:30 a.m. And besides, I was sooooo tired. I apologized to her, suggested that I had found that a vacuum was helpful, and got off that flight vowing *never* to fly again with my children—and never to fly *that* airline.

There was also the nasty young woman at our local sandwich shop. We had literally just moved that day from New Mexico to Kentucky. We were filthy from driving, meeting the truck, and unloading a whole house's worth of stuff. Everything was in boxes, we were all exhausted, and we had to eat. There was a soup and sandwich shop down the street from us, and because it was a chain, we were used to going there. We were all craving something familiar. So, off we went. While waiting for the food, my husband took our son and daughter into the restroom to wash their hands. I could hear the water play and shrieks from where I was sitting halfway across the restaurant. I couldn't even move I was so tired. I stayed there—knowing that I would deal with it when they came out. And besides, it was his turn. When they came back, the children immediately hid under our table with muffled giggles emerging.

This young woman, early 20s in all of her thin cuteness, strode up to my table, and in the most snotty manner said, "I have *never* seen such poorly behaved children in my whole life!" and stalked away in righteous indignation. I just watched her go, angry, tired, and beyond irritated that *she* had clearly never been so tired that her eyelashes hurt.

"Too" Compliant

Although the behaviors often were out of control, there were some things that were not. Elizabeth and Ray never tried to cross streets, poke their fingers in light sockets, or battle for control of cabinets. To this day, they will stop at the corners on their scooters and wait for me to catch up while I'm walking. I certainly didn't mind this overcompliance, because we often have enough battles to worry about, but it did make me wonder when I watched my friends engage in power struggles with their children. We had power struggles, just not the usual kinds. In her book, Susan Senator (2005) also noted how compliant her child was, unless he was screaming and out of control. When autism has hijacked their reactions, children appear unable to control anything, and when they are momentarily in charge of their autism, they can be "too good." There often is very little middle ground.

And Yet . . .

Despite the warning signs of autism, there often are signs of significant strengths that can signal high-functioning autism. "Experts" can watch children and say, "Nope, I don't see autism" because the child is making eye contact, or is listening to you, or is engaging in imaginative play, or is talking—behaviors that often are not found in children with more traditional autism. These are the challenges that families face: there is "something," but what? Giftedness? Autism? Anxiety? Asperger's syndrome? These children often defy easy classification and are ultimately amalgams of many different, overlapping issues.

CALLING TRIPLE A: ASKING FOR HELP

You worry about when you should start worrying. I remember making "appointments" for worrying: "Well, I'll pay attention to her language in a month; we'll see how she's doing then." When you start suspecting something might be wrong, you will look for either confirmation that you're crazy or you'll check in with the professionals—who will probably tell you you're crazy.

I first started asking the pediatrician about concerns of mine at about 16 months. Elizabeth wasn't talking. She wasn't babbling, she wasn't even making much noise, other than a pleased hum when she was happy and an ear-piercing shriek when she wasn't. She *was* however, *very* athletic. She could walk at 9 months, climb slides at 11 months, and was trying to swim at a year. The pediatrician listened to my concerns at 16 months and then smiled and said something like, "Oh well, children develop at their own individual rates. She's obviously spent so much energy on physically growing up—she'll catch up."

I was *livid* when a mere 8 months later, at 2 years old, the pediatrician asked very casually, "Does she have 50 to 100 words in her vocabulary?" I just looked at her and said, "She has about five words, and four of them are only words that we can understand." The pediatrician then said, "Oh, that IS a problem!" In her defense, she was using checklists given to her by the American Association of Pediatricians and autism was less on the horizon in 2002 than it is now. And my daughter is considered high functioning—she did not exhibit some of the other characteristics of autism. But I was still angry: I *knew* my daughter and I *knew* that there was a problem. I found my list of her words the other day:

- Mama
- Da: which could mean "Daddy" or "What's that?" based on the context
- Diddle-la: which was a variation of our dog "Cody Dog" and also meant "home"—we always found that sweet

- Ay: for Ray, her brother
- Ee: for Irene, our frequent babysitter

That was it. Five words. No, she did not have 50 words and yes, that was a problem.

The Landscape and Its Signage

2

MAP NAMES—OR ALPHABET SOUP

It would be so much easier if there were some clearly identifiable traits of autism, or even only one kind of it. Down syndrome is relatively easy. There is a genetic marker for it—the 21st chromosome is tripled (typically, we have two copies of this chromosome). There also is a characteristic look among children with Down syndrome. However, even among children with Down syndrome, there are so many levels of development. There are children who never develop language. There are children who grow up to live fairly independently. There are children who can become professional actors (I *loved* the movie *The Ringer* with Johnny Knoxville, which showcases several actors with Down syndrome). It is getting more clearly understood that while genetics are important to autism, there are a whole interaction of events that take place in order to trigger it. Although

evidence is mounting up that there is a genetic link to autism, it is still identified through observed behavior, not a DNA sequencing test. Thus, depending on how a child acts or behaves and how severe these behaviors might be, there are a variety of labels that might be applied.

Many mothers will use what Jenny McCarthy calls the University of Google. This can be supplemented by what I call the "University of Wikipedia" and the various small "colleges" of blogs, books, and organizations' websites. In most of them, you will see terms that keep popping up—terms that you might have seen before, or you thought you knew, but now apply to a different context. It is like learning a new language: the language of autism. The common terms to describe various forms of are autism are listed below and described in the sections that follow:

- autism spectrum disorders (ASDs)
- autism
- Pervasive Developmental Disorder-Not Otherwise Specified (PDD-NOS)
- Childhood Disintegrative Disorder (CDD)
- Asperger's syndrome (AS)
- Rett syndrome

Autism Spectrum Disorders (ASDs)

This is a "blanket" term—it covers a lot of ground and vague characteristics. My child with autism can act, speak, and interact nothing like your child with autism. You can watch two children with autism in the same place and wonder how on Earth these two children could share the same label. There is a phrase I've heard many times: "When you meet one child with autism, you've met one child with autism."

According to the Emory Autism Center (2009), individuals with an autism spectrum disorder are characterized by impairment in three areas of development: communication, socialization, and unusual interests/behaviors. The characteristics of this disorder can range from mild to severe. Likewise, cognitive and adaptive functioning can range from gifted to severely impaired. The autism spectrum disorders do not describe a delay in development, but rather a difference or deviation in development in the above listed areas.

It doesn't help either that there are so many subnames for autism and overlapping terminology. All of them fall under what is called autism spectrum disorder or ASD. To add to the bewildering array of names, sometimes ASD is called Pervasive Developmental Disorders, and can include autism, Pervasive Developmental Disorder-Not Otherwise Specified, and Asperger's syndrome. PDD-NOS is not to be confused with Rett syndrome or Childhood Disintegrative Disorder, but these subcategories *do* fall under ASD. Confused yet?

Boys are four times more like than girls (with the exception of Rett syndrome; see below) to be diagnosed. Essentially, there are five types of ASD, including: (1) autism (also called classic autism), (2) PDD-NOS, (3) Childhood Disintegrative Disorder, (4) Asperger's syndrome, and (5) Rett syndrome. Throughout this book, I will use the term "autism" to describe all of the subtypes of ASD, not just classic autism. When appropriate to distinguish, I will distinguish Asperger's syndrome from the others, because it differs most in the types of symptoms. The others differ in severity and cause.

When I discuss high-functioning autism, I will include all of these labels in the discussion. What I mean by high functioning are children with autistic behaviors who have the capability of interacting, speaking, and learning general education curriculum in a general education classroom environment with the right supports. According to Dr. Dawson and her associates (2007), these children have higher degrees of fluid intelligence rather than the more fixed intelligence related to memory and perception. In some cases, they can be identified as gifted as well, but I will primarily focus on the need to identify and teach to their abilities, rather than focusing on their disabilities.

Autism

Children with classic autism tend to function in the lower levels of intelligence, due in part to their language skills, which may be significantly lower than the other subtypes. In the past, many people with classic autism were institutionalized and many also had significant health or physical issues as well. However, there is a great deal of confusion in terminology between the word "autism" and the broader term "autism spectrum disorders," which often include newer terms for variations of intellectual functioning, language, problem-solving abilities, and times of diagnosis.

Pervasive Developmental Disorder, Not Otherwise Specified (PDD-NOS)

I just love this term. "Not Otherwise Specified" is official language for "We have no idea" and "It's not low enough to be called autism." I call it the "There's a problem in development somewhere, and who the heck knows why?" And it has its own acronym! My daughter had this label. Not very helpful. According to the Emory Autism Center (2009), PDD-NOS is defined as "a general category used to describe a pattern of behavioral differences (which may include deviations, excesses, or difficulties) in the areas of social relating, communication, and attention/interest)" (para. 3). It frequently is considered a milder version of autism.

Childhood Disintegrative Disorder (CDD)

This is perhaps the most heartbreaking of labels and the most rare. According to Dr. Fombonne (2002), only 1 in 100,000 people demonstrate CDD. This truly is where you are in Italy, and in a very short space of time, you are lifted into Holland. This term describes children who develop typically, and then around 3 to 4 years of age begin to regress—to disintegrate—right before your eyes. Children with this form of autism typically end up with more severe forms: very limited language, very limited social skills, and behaviors that are "classically" autistic. This is the version that most people think of when they think of autism.

Asperger's Syndrome (AS)

This term is used to describe children who are on the autism spectrum, but do not have language delay, although they may have communication differences. However, they do have the social issues and often have the repetitive behaviors and sensory sensitivities of other children on the spectrum. It is a relatively new diagnostic term that was not included in the autism spectrum until 1995. Thus, most people identified as having AS are still under the age of 25. Many parents and grandparents will not have heard of it.

Often, children with AS aren't identified until late elementary or even middle school, although more severe cases do tend to get identified earlier. And, as I can attest to in my friendship with Sam, there are a large number of functioning adults who weren't identified but clearly have it. Sam could have an amazingly interesting conversation with people one-on-one with fascinating insights into politics, humor, and pop culture. He could quote entire episodes of *Seinfeld* that made us laugh. But put him at a party, and he would barricade me into a corner to talk about the same subjects one-on-one and not perceive the subtle social cues of shifting feet, "OK, well, that's interesting, but . . . ," and yawns. These children often grow up to become "geeks" and other not-so-nice labels. It is important to remember that it *is* a problem, and AS does not just represent overlabeling by protective mothers as some believe. It is equally important to realize that there are significant strengths that need focus and specialized development in order to grow.

It is important to note that at the time of this writing, according to Claudia Wallis of *The New York Times*, the American Psychiatric Association (APA) was considering removing both the terms Asperger's syndrome and PDD-NOS from the 2012 revised edition of the *Diagnostic and Statistical Manual for Mental Disorders* (*DSM*)—the definitive book for mental health diagnoses followed by most professionals. Because of the vagueness of both terms, they announced plans to more explicitly define the term autism spectrum to include severity scales, and incorporate the issues faced by people with both PDD-NOS and Asperger's under the ASD category.

Rett Syndrome

This is a known genetic mutation on the X chromosome that can cause significant "autistic-like" behaviors and almost always occurs in girls. It is very rare, occurring only in 1 out of 10,000 to 15,000 people, according to the National Institute of Mental Health (2001). It also can be confused with cerebral palsy, because a child's walking gait and movements can be spastic or jerky. Children often will have small heads and have little language abilities. They also have seizures and digestive issues. Children with Rett syndrome often will behave in ways similar to children with autism, but there is a known cause for their actions. It is not considered inherited, because it seems to be a genetic mutation that occurs randomly.

OTHER MAPS—OTHER COUNTRIES: OVERLAPPING DISORDERS

There are lots of other issues that children with autism may have as well. These are called "comorbid disorders," and there appears to be some form of link between these and autism, but researchers haven't found the linkages yet. I tend to think of them all as a vast Venn diagram with overlapping circles of characteristics (see Figure 2), with some children having some of the symptoms, and some not.

Febrile Seizures/Epilepsy

Many children with autism have seizures in which their brain goes through a small series of electric shocks. Rachel, the mother of a child with autism, experienced this when her child became sick:

> It was a very hot and busy day and I was treating him with Tylenol every 4 hours. His grandmother was holding him while I ran a cool bath for him. Suddenly he began to shake all over, his eyes rolled up into his head, and he went limp. I thought he had died.

Figure 2. Overlapping circles, representing the overlapping symptoms of autism and other disorders.

He was out for more than a few minutes and taken to the hospital. When we got there, his temperature was around 104, and I knew from how he felt earlier that this was cooler. His actual maximum temperature was never determined and therefore, it's unclear as to the damage it may have done.

Doctors are quick to reassure parents that febrile seizures are not life-threatening and can happen many times in a child's life. However, there is such a link between these types of brain seizures and autism that I have to believe that there must be some form of impact.

Digestive Issues

There are some very interesting research studies that have found links between autism and the digestive system at a chromosomal level. Many parents can tell you about their child's "leaky gut" in which their child does not develop well physically, nor do they digest food well. Chronic constipation and diarrhea are common issues among children with autism. According to Shaw and colleagues (1998), there often is an overabundance of yeast and opioids in the digestive tracts of children with autism and a decreased level of necessary proteins. Similarly, phenylketonuria, or PKU, often is confused with autism because of the similar behaviors. Children with PKU are missing a key digestive enzyme that left untreated can lead to problems in brain development. In most states, infants are automatically screened for PKU with blood tests conducted right after birth, but it is important to know if your child was or not. Celiac disease often is suspected in many children with autism as well, as gluten-free diets appear to work so well in both populations.

Tourette's Syndrome

Tourette's is a genetic disorder noticed when the child develops a tic or physical and vocal movements associated with stress. The version that most people think of is the more extreme one where people shout obscenities and make highly inappropriate remarks. In reality, there are lots of children and adults with Tourette's who do nothing more than clear their throats and blink their eyes when they're anxious. However, tics can fall under repetitive behaviors, so there are many children who meet criteria for both autism and Tourette's and there appears to be a certain amount of overlap. Dr. John Walkup (2006) noted that he gets more children with Asperger's syndrome in his Tourette's clinic at Johns Hopkins University than the university's AS clinic. In addition, Tourette's can be influenced by stress and anxiety, conditions that can aggravate autistic behaviors as well.

Anxiety Disorders

Many children with social problems act out when they are placed in situations where they have to talk with other people. According to the National Institute of Mental Health (2008), up to 18% of the general population may have anxiety disorders. Adults and children can get headaches, exhaustion, or muscle spasms. Some people with anxiety disorders have problems maintaining physical balance—an interesting correlation to their inability to maintain mental balance. My son, Raymond, has anxiety disorder and Tourette's syndrome, and when he is going somewhere new, or something has happened in his life to disrupt his schedule, he will grunt, avoid eye contact, and be unable to eat. Obsessive-Compulsive Disorders (OCD) can fall under anxiety disorders as well, so there are overlaps of all kinds of issues.

Sleep Disorders

Many children with autism experience sleep disorders, sleeping little at night, having bedwetting episodes, and being tired throughout the day. Colic among babies is common for an extended period of time and can last for years. Recent studies have found a link between lack of sleep and a large number of disorders, including autism and ADHD. This is true around the world (see Taira, Takase, & Sasaki, 2008).

A friend of mine has had her son in many sleep studies trying to figure out how to get him to sleep well. "I would give anything for a decent night's sleep," she says. "When by some miracle, he does sleep, everything is better—for all of us." The professionals' recommendation? Get more sleep. Have an established sleep routine. I was so annoyed for her! It's a chicken and egg argument. Does autism cause the sleep disorder or does the lack of sleep aggravate autism? I certainly know that when Elizabeth experiences sleeplessness, her autistic tendencies increase and her language skills markedly decline. We laugh in our family that we can tell when she's tired—she starts talking about herself in the third person ("Elizabeth wants popcorn"). Her pronouns decline dramatically. She falls more often. But we are lucky: She does tend to sleep well, but needs lots of it.

Intellectual Disabilities (Mental Retardation)

Having difficulties with language, many children with autism are unable to communicate their needs or questions. They can behave in ways that seem much younger than their actual physical age. Most commonly found in classic autism or CDD, the overlap with intellectual disabilities (formerly known as mental retardation) raises the issue of language because the ability to determine actual intelligence of a child who is unable to communicate with others is challenging. Intellectual disabilities can be found in anywhere from 25%–70% of children with classic autism, according to the Autism Society (2009).

Learning Disabilities

Because of the delay in language or inability to understand others' perspectives, reading and comprehension scores can lag significantly behind age peers for some children on the spectrum. Reading comprehension is a typical problem where the child can "word call" (or read words in isolation) but is not able to determine the meaning of the piece or make connections between readings.

Giftedness

Because some children on the spectrum learn to read and do math at very young ages, they can be gifted in many areas. Because of their ability to focus, long attention spans, and deep interest in a subject, many children with high-functioning autism also are gifted. There is a significant overlap between Asperger's syndrome and gifted behaviors, according to Jim Webb and his colleagues (2005). Most children with autism and giftedness tend to prefer nonfiction and scientific topics and will explore the content in-depth in their particular area of interest. Giftedness to the level that is identified by a school district is not common, but it is a possibility.

Weakened Immune Systems

Many children with autism almost appear to have an allergic reaction to their lives. Their immune systems are compromised and they often are unable to fight off colds, allergies, and other illnesses. According to Drs. Konstantareas and Homatidis (1987), ear infections appear to be more rampant among children who eventually get diagnosed with autism and many parents report that their children were given frequent doses of antibiotics when they were babies. It is not clear if the immune system issues are a cause of, or a result from, the autism or linked through genetic relationships.

SPEAKING THE LINGO— DESCRIBING YOUR CONCERNS

My goal in this section is for you to have some language to use when you're trying to get someone to listen or to help. When you're first aware that something's "just not right," how do you move beyond that vague concern to making a professional listen? Your mother-in-law, your babysitter, your sister—they all know that something is not quite right, but how do you describe it?

Official Language

There's a whole host of official jargon that you will have to plow your way through. When I teach college freshmen to start speaking "educational-ese," I teach them to think of it like learning another language. Autism has yet again a whole new set of words to learn. Words you thought you knew the meanings of don't quite mean the same thing in this new journey. This is not even close to an exhaustive list, but it's a starting point for you. For more information, please seek out more specific texts, or check with the professionals with whom you work.

Typical and Atypical

These are words to describe what *most* children do at a specific age in a specific time and place. It is important to not think of them as normal and not normal, although most people do. Normal implies judgment—something you want your child to be. It is considered *typical* of a 4-year-old child who is moving from one city to another to act out and cry while he or she is in the grocery store. However, is acting out and crying considered *normal* when he or she is in the grocery store? Normal doesn't really take

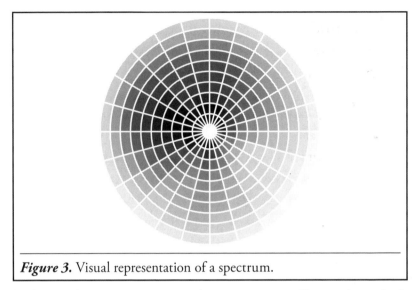

Figure 3. Visual representation of a spectrum.

background situations into consideration. In typical/atypical, you look for things that aren't really explained by the age or the situation. There are *lots* of young children who act out, scream, or focus on objects, but for how long, at what age, and what else is going on?

Spectrum

Autism is a spectrum disorder, which means that there are degrees of severity among a whole lot of different characteristics (see Figure 3 for a visual representation of a spectrum). There are some children who will exhibit mild characteristics and others with very severe symptoms. There are many children who do not qualify for services who exhibit some of these characteristics, and other children who do qualify who demonstrate very different characteristics from each other. The phrase I often use is "children on the spectrum," which can include all of the various forms of autism, including CDD and "classic" autism on the lower functioning end, Asperger's syndrome and PDD-NOS on the higher functioning end, and Rett syndrome, which can occur across the spectrum of functioning.

Characteristic

The use of this term means that children might show a certain behavior, and that many other children with autism have this same type of behavior. But it may not be enough to qualify for a label, or there may be other significant characteristics that are missing. It's a bit like looking at one puzzle piece and saying, "Yes, that looks like it goes to that puzzle, but without the other pieces, it's hard to say." Children may exhibit autistic-like characteristics and not qualify for autism, but they still act differently.

Criteria

Criteria is the official term for the level of intensity and combination of characteristics that have to be there to qualify for the label (in order to be treated or receive services). Criteria do not imply severity; just that according to an outside authority, the child meets the standards for that label on multiple characteristics. For example, children with social impairments and repetitive behaviors but without language delays might fit the criteria for Asperger's syndrome, but not for PDD-NOS.

Dysfunction

Dysfunction means that something does not work well or the way it's supposed to for others of the same age. Social dysfunction means that children don't socialize the way that other children do. It's a global term that tries to take out the judgmental aspect without going all the way to the term disorder. According to my husband and mother, I have an organizational dysfunction, but it's not a significant problem for me. It may be annoying for my husband, who has to see my bedside table piled with things that I'm doing at the time—a sewing project, three books, several cards in process of writing, random earrings I took off and didn't take back to the jewelry box, and so on—but it's not a real problem in my life. I can find things I need to and my life is not deeply affected. Still, a dysfunction *can* become a disorder or disability if it gets too significant in a person's life.

Disorder

Disorder implies that the ability that is impaired is creating a significant problem in a person's life. However, disorders are not assumed to be permanent and can sometimes be "cured" given appropriate treatment or developmental growth. However, it is important to know that treatment for a disorder is not an equation—there is never one known "right" way. There may be many, many strategies and treatments available that may or may not be effective for a particular child.

Disability

Disability means that there is a dysfunction that creates significant problems for a child, and it is assumed to be a permanent situation. However, although it may be permanent, there are still strategies and techniques that can help the child learn to cope. Many people have learning disabilities or behavior disabilities, and they can be taught to cope with them. I teach my prospective teachers that you can't teach someone to overcome his disability, but you can teach him how to learn *around* it or cope with it. An example of a disability would be someone with artificial limbs. He can learn to run again with a prosthetic leg, but he can't ignore the fact that his original leg is missing. Someone with a learning disability can learn to cope and function, but she can't ignore the fact that she learns differently.

Handicap

Handicap is the old term for disability, but there is an underlying assumption that the condition cannot get better. Thus, you have handicap parking because the problem that created the need for a person to need to park close to a store is not going to get better. My college sweetheart's mother had a handicapped sticker because she had a serious heart condition. That heart condition could not be "taught" to get better.

High Functioning Versus Low Functioning

There are no clear-cut differences between high-functioning and low-functioning children with autism. The informal understanding is that children who are high functioning have stronger language and problem-solving skills, and have slightly below-average to above-average intelligence. There is a tremendous overlap with both Asperger's syndrome and PDD-NOS. According to Happé (1999), children with high-functioning autism have a different cognitive style, not ability, and score higher on fluid intelligence tests. Children who are low functioning tend to have characteristics that are more severe, lower language, lower intelligence scores, and often have other issues as well. Traditionally, Asperger's syndrome and PDD-NOS are considered higher functioning, while CDD and "classic" autism are lower, but these labels can vary widely from child to child. When I describe my daughter as high functioning, I am trying to imply that she is on or above grade level in most academic subjects, still struggles with language to some degree, still has some sensory and social issues, and you might not even know that she had autism if you met her. My friend Tara's nephew, who is low functioning, has very limited language, just got potty trained at age 11, and is in a self-contained classroom in his school. There are lots of children in between, above and below them, but all of them have autism and yet all of them are unique.

There also is a greater chance of high-functioning children "recovering" from autism. According to a 2009 study by Dr. Fein and colleagues, between 10%–20% of children diagnosed with high-functioning autism between the ages of 1 and 3 no longer qualified as having autism by the age of 9. Some parents and methods claim that autism can be "cured," but it would appear from Dr. Fein's work, as well as work by Dr. Kogan from the CDC (2009), that children with high-functioning autism who receive intensive early therapy are better able to overcome many of the debilitating issues they face.

Behavioral Terminology

There are essentially five ways you can describe a child's behavior. Use the terms correctly, and you've gained instant credibility from a professional. These also will help you explain to your mother or your grandmother what the difference is between your child's behavior and "spoiled." It is important to know that the visible difference between a spoiled child and a child on the spectrum is in your responses to the behavior; if you are consistent, firm, and follow through on natural consequences, then the problem is your child's response to good parenting. Of course, that then places the burden back on you to prove your child's problems, and not be blamed for them, because the tantrums that a child on the spectrum can throw can look an awful lot like the tantrum of a child whose parent is too tired and too unwilling to be the enforcer. Much of the difference lies in what appears to *cause* the problem—is it manipulation of the situation or being overwhelmed by the situation? Are they engaging in a power struggle with you, or are they searching for power of any kind because they feel so out of control? It often is very difficult to determine the difference and to describe the differences. But if you *know* that you're doing the best you can, ask for help and use the vocabulary below to assist you.

- *Characteristics*: What does something *look* like? It's a way of describing *what* a child is doing: What words are being used? What expression is on her face? Lots of kids want to go swimming. When Elizabeth was 5 and we were at a party, she fixated on the fact that there was a pool there, it was warm, and she wanted to go swimming. Never mind the fact that she had no suit and no one else was swimming. (We were at my office party.) Every word out of her mouth was about swimming for the whole party until she said, "I can't stop thinking about it!"
- *Frequency*: How *often* does a certain behavior occur? For example, as I was keeping track of her vocabulary, I noted that my daughter said the word "mommy" twice in one day. You'll have to count and keep track of how many times a behavior occurs.

- *Latency*: How long after you ask for a certain behavior does a child do it? For example, how long does it take to get him to respond to his name? Typical kids will respond immediately to their name. Our friend Gus sometimes would appear to have to think about what his name meant before he would turn toward you.
- *Duration*: How *long* does a behavior last? My son doesn't throw tantrums often: once every 4 to 6 months. The frequency of tantrums is low. But when he does . . . phew! His tantrum record is 3 1/2 hours. That's 3 ½ hours of shrieking, hurling himself about, and repeating the same statement over and over again.
- *Intensity*: How loud or soft, or hard, or big or small does the behavior occur? What is the size of the behavior? It's one thing to shut the door. It's a whole other thing to *slam* the door. Middle school kids are prone to issues of intensity and when you fuss at them, the response typically is "WHAT? I was JUST (dropping my books, closing the door, getting out a pencil, setting the table . . . name it)." Intensity has to do with degrees. It's typical behavior, that's just, well, more intense.

POTENTIAL DETOUR SIGNS

So, given all of these overlapping names and types and other issues and words, what *are* you looking for? What behavior are you trying to describe? Autism and other spectrum disorders are diagnosed when there is a problem in three areas:
- language delay or communication problems,
- repetitive behaviors, and
- social problems.

Although not often part of the official diagnostic criteria, the following characteristics are noted among kids with high-functioning autism.
- sensory under- or overstimulation,

- visual learning styles,
- physical issues, and
- discrepant academic abilities.

There are variations of these. Children with Asperger's syndrome tend not to have language delays, but do have significant social impairment. Children with PDD-NOS tend not to be as low on all of these characteristics as a child with classic autism or CDD. Children with epilepsy or intestinal disorders also may have other physical symptoms.

But what do these *look* like? Not every child is going to exhibit all of these. And many children without autism exhibit some of these characteristics, and many of these characteristics overlap with other exceptionalities, including giftedness. But look at the list *holistically*—is there more than one characteristic that is significant? Do they cause a problem, rather than just being a trait? Does your gut instinct tell you something is wrong? Most importantly, do you worry? If you do, it's worth checking out.

There are several characteristics of autism spectrum disorders to look for and to be able to describe to your doctor/therapists. Your child may not exhibit all of them, but you need to be able to describe them; either to say, "No, my child doesn't do this," or to say, "This is what I'm seeing." For more information on helping you spot characteristics of autism, *please* go to a more in-depth source. This is *not* meant to provide significant information—just an overview of some of the more common issues. I have listed several sites for you in the Resources section of this book that should be helpful.

Language Usage

Language is the most significant characteristic of children on the spectrum. What they say, how they say it, and when they talk can be affected. However, it also is one of the hardest issues to get anyone to help you with. Before the age of 2, there are so few words that most children say, so much room for individual differences, and so many myths about how children talk:

- Boys talk later than girls.
- His dad/our neighbor/Einstein didn't talk until he was 3/4/when he was good and ready (many, many variations of this one).
- The ear infections could be an issue.
- They're developing in other ways; language will catch up.

Some of these myths are rooted in reality—children *do* develop in highly individual manners. My first child walked at 9 months; my second at 13 months. Both are well within the range of "normal" for that developmental milestone. But, if you have questions or concerns, see a professional. A delay may be just that—a delay that the child will overcome on her own. But a significant delay may need some assistance to overcome. And language forms the foundation of almost all learning, a critical process to further development.

Language Problems

Language problems can range from delayed, to nonexistent, to blurry, to just strange usage. And it's important to recognize that language is not just spoken language, but the whole process of communication—facial expressions, gestures, body language, and reactivity.

Nonverbal language usage is a key trait to verbal language. Many children on the spectrum do not use nonverbal gestures, such as pointing, to communicate. Karyn Seroussi (2002) shared how excited she was that her son was learning how to point, until the therapist said that typical children don't *have* to be taught how to point—they do it automatically.

Echolalia is a frequent issue with kids with autism. They will repeat things that they hear either immediately afterward or quite a while afterward. The key is that they are repeating what someone else has said, not generating unique phraseology on their own. Elizabeth, when she didn't know the answer to a question, would pull something out of her repertoire—often something she heard on television. I would ask her what the weather was doing outside, and I would get a few sentences from the newscast the night before. We used her ability for echolalia to teach her scripts: "When someone says this, 'How are you, Elizabeth?' You say 'Fine.'" A friend of mine's son, who is lower functioning, particularly loves Elmo, even though he's 8, and will provide you sentences from "Elmo's World" when you try to engage him in conversation.

Echolalia can be sneaky. You might think that children with autism are having a conversation, or even talking to themselves, until you realize that they're feeling the words around in their mouth, almost from an experiential sensory process. Recently, my son was fascinated to learn what the "F" word was. I had told him that I wasn't going to teach him what it was, but when he thought he knew what it was, to come and talk to me about it. On a class field trip, an oh-so-helpful boy in his class taught him the full range of George Carlin's Seven Words. Ray popped into the car that afternoon, full of questions and asked, "Mommy, is the F word F—k?" Ahhh . . . the end of innocence.

"Yes, Ray it is . . ." I said sadly, realizing my son had made an important vocabulary leap, followed by a full-on parental lecture on why we never, *ever* say that word. Ray listened politely. I then heard him whispering the word, rolling it around in his mouth, feeling it out, trying different emphases and tones.

"Huh," he said, disappointedly. "I thought it would be longer."

Words are sensory things. The short bark of the "F word" is short, sharp, and harsh. The rhythm of the word "Savannah" has long been a favorite of mine with its cadence and relaxed mouth muscles. Kids with autism will feel the words in their mouth, and often completely ignore the meaning behind them.

Echolalia also is a word-finding strategy, but as Mize and Hensler (2008) noted, it is a positive sign as it demonstrates that the child is using language for communication purposes—he or she just has no idea what words to use. Children who do not have a strong grasp on finding or understanding words may reach for what they've heard before, or, more likely, learned on television or heard from others close to them. They do not understand the question, or cannot find an appropriate response, and so in an effort to remain engaged, will parrot back something that caught their attention at an earlier time. The frustrating thing is that echolalia really is a desperate strategy of staying engaged, but it ends up cutting off conversation as the other person has nowhere to go.

Interestingly, music seems to play a role in echolalia with its ability to help kids remember words. Many kids with autism will be able to sing back television theme songs or repeat music heard off of the radio. For reasons we don't quite yet understand, music is processed in the brain in a location different than the place where language is processed. Therefore, it can be more accessible at times when words are not available. Studies, such as Dr. Oldfield's (2006) in Australia, found that music decreased echolalic and "acting out" behaviors.

With no musical ability at all, we have learned to sing and chant things that Elizabeth and Ray need to remember on the days that they are not overwhelmed by the "noise" of music. The morning schedule? Posted visually and sung to them. "This is the way we clean our room, clean our room, clean our room . . . We put clothes away, clothes away, clothes away . . . We make our bed, make our bed, make our bed . . ." I will hear them humming it as they (badly) make up their beds. Some issues, such as messy rooms, are just not unique to kids with autism.

Dyspraxia/Apraxia

There are many overlapping terms, but all have to do with muscle coordination; in the case of language, dyspraxia is a condition where the tongue muscles are difficult for the child to move smoothly and it requires great effort for the child to make clear sounds. Children with autism can hold onto "baby speech" for far too long. When Elizabeth is tired or hurt, she will call herself "Ewizabeth." It takes great concentration and energy for them to keep their tongues active and toned. "L's and

"R"s, difficult sounds even for typical children, can be very challenging for children with autism.

A symptom of dyspraxia, and perhaps as a result of possible poor neurological connection, is that the child often will put things in his or her mouth. It was explained to me by our speech therapist that a baby's first nerve is the shortest and strongest one from his mouth to the center of his brain. Babies put things into their mouth because that's the first way they learn about things—it's their version of looking at something carefully. They're putting deep pressure on their upper palate, creating a stronger sense of connection and stimulation. Because touch and sight senses develop more slowly, they really do "know" things first by the way they feel in their mouth. Kids with autism often have scrambled sight and touch senses, so their mouth remains their best way of learning about the world. All I knew is that Elizabeth had a very difficult time stopping her pacifier, and I was always pulling things out of her mouth. Choking was a constant fear of mine. Even now, when she's tired, she'll start sucking on her hair. My friend Tina's son still sucks his thumb at age 13. We always have gum on hand in our house to keep Elizabeth's mouth occupied with a socially acceptable activity. Sucking is both a means of soothing stress as well as exploration and stimulation in all children; it's just that this soothing and exploration continues in children with autism.

According to speech therapist Valerie DeJean (2006), dyspraxia is found in poor muscle tone and poor muscle planning in movements beyond speaking. Children with autism often do not perceive their body as completely as they should and so can have a symptomatic gait or stiff-legged walk. Poor muscle tone can show up in other ways as well. Ray has terrible handwriting because he does not hold a pencil firmly enough. He can stand straight up, but his whole body is sort of "noodle-y." Buttons and zippers can be extremely problematic. Children with autism know how to manipulate them, but not their purpose or how to make them achieve their purpose. Brandon's mother complains about how difficult it is to find shoes for her 13-year-old son because he needs them to fasten with Velcro™. He does not have the physical dexterity to tie his shoes.

Dyspraxia also relates to these children's ability to perceive things in space relative to other things. For example, they can spin the wheels on a car, but they don't understand how that is representative of a car going down the road. Thus, when asked to "make the car go," they experience frustration.

Problems With Pronouns

We can tell when Elizabeth is having a particularly problematic day because she starts talking about herself in the third person: "Elizabeth wants to go play." For some reason, perhaps because pronouns are representative of the thing, not the actual thing itself, children with autism can have problems with first- and second-person pronouns, using "he/she" for "I" or "I" for "you," and confusing gender pronouns with each other.

Global vs. Specific Terms

Children on the spectrum often don't understand "umbrella terms" or words that mean a series of actions, rather than one specific thing. They have challenges making generalizations between one activity and how it might relate to other activities.

The other day I made Elizabeth cry when I called to her to "come clean the kitchen." She just stood and looked at me and I thought that she was being willful—a very strong possibility. "Clean up the kitchen, Elizabeth!" I repeated.

"What do you mean, mommy?"

"I mean clean the kitchen!"

"I don't understand."

"What don't you understand? I told you to go and clean the kitchen, and I mean *now!*"

Prolific tears then came: "What do you mean by 'clean'? What am I supposed to do?"

Guilty! Bad mommy moment. I looked down at my daughter who had just taken the "Big Girl" responsibility a few months before of washing the dishes and realized that she didn't know that that was synonymous with "cleaning." I had to take a deep breath and explain that "clean" is a large, vague term for wiping down the counter, rinsing the dishes . . . all of those small tasks that involve cleaning. Elizabeth often has problems with global terms such as "check your work," "clean your room," "go play," "be nice," "use your manners," and "Are you finished?" There are so many parenting admonishments and questions that are too vague for her to understand. She often gets in trouble at school for similar things. She lives in a world of specifics.

Concepts are particularly hard for children with autism. Concepts are vague and include many other skills in them. Because children with autism often don't generalize, they aren't sure what specific skills are being called for when they're asked to do something.

It is important to note that this need for specificity can sometimes be an area of strength. Often these traits can lead to a deep fascination with computers and math. After all, computers are as precise as they are and math is the process of quantifying things!

Word Finding

Finding the right word for the right situation often can be a challenge for children with autism. They use vague words like "stuff" or "that," or phrases designed to fill in conversational gaps such as "You know." When asked to tell backstories or events, they have a hard time retelling them.

There are times I can almost see the wheels working in Elizabeth's head as she searches for what it is that she wants to tell me. There are a great many websites out there about how children with Asperger's syndrome and autism feel like they are from another planet, aliens if you will. Although I certainly don't believe that my daughter is the result of an alien abduction, as some conspiracy theorists believe is the case about "aspies" (she looks entirely too much like me *and* my husband for me to believe this!), listening to her search for words is somewhat like listening to someone who is learning English as second language. The easy familiarity with the language is not there, and so there is a translation effort that occurs as she works incredibly hard to communicate with others around her.

Lack of Imagination

Because imagination is formed when a child can generalize beyond the here and now into a hypothetical realm, children on the spectrum often have a great deal of trouble with imagination. Hypothetical situations, estimating, and other broad thinking activities tend to be very difficult for these children. They often can see things in black and white, and complex issues are very difficult to understand.

My daughter didn't know what to make of it when our local Nature Center was encouraging children to make fairy houses. She was very confused because she *knew* that fairies did not exist, and yet, here were grownups telling her that they did. She assumed that she was wrong and went around looking for fairies. She wasn't confused between imaginary and real—she just didn't understand what imaginary was.

Hyperlexia

Hyperlexia is a condition where a child develops a precocious ability to read, often along with a fascination of letters and numbers far above their age peers. However, as opposed to giftedness where advanced reading is characteristic, hyperlexia has a corresponding problem of language usage or verbal understanding. Thus, children with hyperlexia have very strong word-calling skills, but often cannot tell you what it is that they've read. Or, conversely, as is the case of children with Asperger's syndrome, according to Lynn Richman (1997) from the Hyperlexia Association, they can understand what they read, but cannot understand something told to them. They also have great challenges summarizing what it is that they have read. Hyperlexia often is paired with autistic behaviors.

My family has a history of thinking in visual words. That means that when we talk, we have to *see* it first in our mind. We laugh about how people cannot tell us directions, we have to see it written down. It is a learning style that is shared with other people, but is a very strong one in my family. Consequently, we read a lot and I read a tremendous amount to Elizabeth and Ray, trying to create emotional and physical connections, as well as developing concepts through books. For example, I bought *The Berenstain Bears Visit the Dentist* to prepare them for their first dentist visit. We understand things when they're in a book and it helps ease the anxiety produced by the experiencing of it.

Although I wasn't intentionally doing it, using hyperlexia often can be a method of therapy. Reading aloud to a child a book as she reads along is a means of allowing her to connect the visual with the auditory, thereby reinforcing the process of language. In his 2000 book, *The Mind Tree*, Tito Mukhopadhyay, a child with autism who is hyperlexic and wrote the book when he was 8 years old, shared the insight he got when he finally realized that "the voices related to people and lips" (p. 16).

Pedantic

Many children on the spectrum can have excellent language skills and have fantastic vocabularies. However, they also can have very little emotion in their voice or face when talking and will use "fancy" words, when simpler words might be more appropriate. They can be called "little professors" (which I find funny and irritating, my being a professor and all).

I can always tell when my husband is stressed—he will start using words that are multisyllabic and precise. I believe that the pedantic language is an attempt to control the chaos that they feel when they are in a stressful situation and are trying to get a precise understanding of it for themselves, without really paying attention to the needs of their audience.

Social Problems

Certainly social problems often are caused by and worsened by the language problems. When children can't find the words for a given situation and can't communicate their needs and wants, everyone can get frustrated. But there are several characteristic social behaviors of children with autism.

Lack of Obvious Emotion or "Flat Affect"

Affect is considered to be the visual representation of responsiveness and emotions: the smile, the frown, the eye contact. This is probably one of the most significant characteristics of autism. Children with autism just don't look or act like most people do when emotions are involved.

Gus was an 8-year old boy I knew with Asperger's syndrome who was obsessed about his cat, Sunny. He wrote stories about Sunny, talked nonstop about Sunny, and would give you detailed information you really didn't want to know about Sunny (I well remember the day that Gus told me all about Sunny throwing up). Then, one Tuesday, Gus started talking about trains. He was telling me about speeds, and types, and histories . . . everything I ever wanted to know and more about trains. I was surprised and amused that within a day's time, Gus could find a new fixation. I told his mother that afternoon, "Looks like Gus got off his obsession with Sunny and moved on to trains."

"Sunny died last night. He got out and was run over by a car. Gus saw it happen," his mom told me, with tears in her eyes.

I was shocked! I had no indication at all that Sunny had died in such a horrific manner, or that Gus had witnessed it. With any other child, I would have expected him to tell me, to express sorrow, to be terribly upset. However, Gus gave every impression of not caring at all about it. Because I knew Gus before I knew much about autism, I was rather disturbed at his apparent callousness and lack of connection to this pet that I assumed that he loved. I made the assumption, that many people do, that people with autism do not feel emotion.

The opposite is true in many cases, however. Often, people with autism care *so* deeply that they don't know how to deal with it. The power of the emotion overwhelms them and they shut it down. What appears to be callousness or negativity actually is a coping mechanism. They may appear not to have emotion, when what they're doing is stuffing down intense emotion that then releases itself in a tantrum or torrent of tears or extreme agitation or hides through a lack of response.

When my son Ray first meets people, he refuses to make eye contact. His face shows no emotion and he will answer in single syllables. I have spent so much time explaining to people that "he's shy," when someone says "Hello" to him, and he refuses to answer. People tend to forgive "shy." They're less forgiving of "He's got an anxiety disorder and you're stressing him out by talking to him."

And yet, he absolutely desires people's positive attention. Raymond craves positive approval so much that when you point out something even moderately negative, he will shut down with a ferocious, withdrawn expression on his face and resort to grunts. However, he cannot tell you what he is feeling. He can't verbalize his feelings of anger or hurt. I have learned to stop my instinctive "No, Ray!" when he is about to do something he shouldn't—reach too high for a glass bowl, walk out into a parking lot without me, or do a problem using addition instead of multiplication—with a question of "Why is that *not* a good idea?" Turning it into an intellectual exercise allows him to deal with the pain of negative attention coming his way.

Lack of Eye Contact

Many children with autism can't make eye contact. The anxiety that they feel when they connect eyes with someone can overwhelm them. They would rather focus on a detail about a person—his shirt, his buttons, anything other than the emotional upheaval of sharing eye gaze. And because they don't process language in quite the same way, they often are unresponsive to their own names. It's as if they just don't hear it as a name or as anything related to themselves. Often, a child not responding to her own name is a trigger for many parents to start to believe something is wrong.

Rozella Stewart (2000), from the Indiana Resource Center for Autism, shared the story told to her by a well-educated man with Asperger's syndrome, who stated that, "If you insist that I make eye contact with you, when I'm finished I'll be able to tell you how many millimeters your pupils changed while I looked into your eyes." Eye contact is so invasive to their psyche, most people with high-functioning autism can't do it. And yet because of the communication component needed by typical people, developing eye contact is one of the first, and hardest, things that therapists focus on in behavior and communication goals. Being able to look people in the eye is a key first step of communication.

Inappropriate or Delayed Interactions

Often it seems as though children with autism try to learn the social codes without truly understanding how or why they work. For example, Gus did not understand the concept or need for personal space. He would be so excited about what he was talking about that he would creep closer and closer to you until he was literally inches from you. He would be gesturing wildly, and the person to whom he was talking would be inching away looking very uncomfortable. One day, Gus made me laugh when he implemented a strategy he had obviously been taught. He was chattering about something, probably trains, when he stopped himself, and said quietly, "arm's distance," and carefully measured the distance from me using his arm. He then looked at me for approval, and was off and chattering again. *He* didn't feel the need to be an arm's distance away from his audience, but he had been taught exactly how far he needed to be in order to make other people comfortable. He was learning the code, without completely understanding the reason for it.

My son appears to have understood the code for children his own age quite well. He plays games well and has a great sense of imagination. My daughter? Not so much . . .

One day, my 4-year-old son had his best friend, a 5-year-old girl, over to play at the park. "Let's play dinosaurs," my son enthusiastically suggested.

"Let's play house," she replied.

"Let's play dinosaur house!" he retorted, and within minutes, they were setting up rocks as a Tyrannosaurus rex's house, and he was running about to steal eggs for dinner. She was the dinosaur mama and was cooking the stolen eggs while he busily defended the home with ferocious teeth. Beyond the obvious sexism, I was deeply amused at how Ray was able to combine two games of play into a game agreeable to all and to truly live his play.

Meanwhile, 5-year-old Elizabeth had been swinging and gradually wandered over to the action. "Mama, I want to play," she told me.

"So, go play with them, honey. They're good at figuring out things to do."

So Elizabeth went and stood stock still in the middle of their "kitchen." "Will you play with me?" she said in a plaintive tone.

"Sure!" replied her brother. "You can be Sister Dinosaur!"

"I don't want to play dinosaurs," she whined. Ray shrugged and zoomed off with arms widespread, turning into a velociraptor. All dragging arms and droopy eyes, Elizabeth came back to me crying: "They won't play with me, Mommy!"

Oh my darling girl: How do I, as an adult, help her navigate the strange world of 5-year-olds? I suggested that she invite them to climb the play structure when she stopped crying. That time it worked, but later? As a 10-year-old? Lord help us, as a 13-year-old? And as a 16-year-old starting to fall in love? Ah me . . .

Theory of Mind

There is a developmental step called "theory of mind" that develops in most children around age 4. They can understand that what they can see and think and feel is not necessarily what other people can see and think and feel.

There is a famous test, devised by Dr. Simon Baron-Cohen (see Baron-Cohen & Leslie, 1985), called the "Sally and Anne" test, where you can test to see if children have reached this understanding. Essentially, the child is presented with two dolls named Sally and Anne, a bucket, a basket, and a story that is carried out using the dolls. The child is told that the dolls are playing and that they hide a marble in a basket. Sally then goes for a walk. While she is gone, Anne moves the marble into the bucket. When Sally returns, the child is asked, "Where does Sally think the marble is?" If the child has theory of mind, the child will understand that even though he or she knows that the marble is in the bucket, Sally thinks that the marble is in the basket. If the child does not have theory of mind, he or she will fully believe that Sally thinks that the marble is where the child knows it was moved. He or she will be unable to understand that other people do not know or are not interested in the information or beliefs that they have.

Most children develop theory of mind around age 4 naturally and cannot be hurried into it. I remember trying to teach my 2-year-old son this concept. He was looking at a picture book in his car seat in the backseat while I was driving. "What's that?" he asked, pointing to the book.

"I don't know, Ray. I can't see it," I responded.

"That, *right there*!" he insisted.

"I can't see it, sweetheart. I'm looking forward, you're looking at it. I can't tell you because I can't see it."

He then proceeded to have a complete meltdown right then because he just knew that I was holding out information on him. It was a learning experience for me about the power of developmental thought and how important it was to be able to understand other's perspectives.

Often, children with Asperger's syndrome will not be able to fully demonstrate theory of mind. They do not understand that other people are not as fascinated with geology, trains, animals, space, or whatever they currently are involved with. They do not understand why other people behave or feel differently than they do. They are unable to understand other people's reactions to them other than as an intellectual problem. This trait also can be found in gifted children who also can have strong interests and express frustration that other children do not understand or follow their rules. However, in most gifted children, they are advanced in their developmental process and are thinking like children much older than they are and are frustrated at their peers' inability to think at the same level.

There is a characteristic look in the eyes of children with autism that I can now recognize. It's a bit of a "lost" look as they look out from eyes that want to engage, want to belong, but aren't quite sure how. They are strangers in a strange land and are trying to figure out how these other people work.

Repetitive Behaviors

Repetitive behaviors is a pretty broad term for actions that are done over and over again for the purpose of soothing or stimulating. Sometimes they're easy to recognize: rocking of the body, head banging, and flapping of arms. They can also be verbal: hooting, humming, or whooping. It is *very* important to know that repetitive behaviors are ways that all people deal with stressful situations, both positive stress and negatives stress. We all know people who eat, tap pencils, jiggle their legs, chew their fingernails, and twiddle their thumbs. It's not the process of moving that is a characteristic, but both the intensity of the repetitions and the cultural appropriateness of the situation. Many people hum to themselves when they're standing in line or bored. But most do not hum during a business meeting. Many people will clap their hands or shake them when they're excited about something, but most don't flap their whole hands or arms. According to the Watson Institute (2005), repetitive movements tend to appear in children with autism around age 2 and peak around age 4.

Lines

Parents often first notice their child's autistic-like behaviors when the child lines up toys, sorting by color or some criteria unknown to the watching parent. Aaron, a friend's son, would arrange his toy vehicles according to function: road workers first, mass transportation second, cars third, and "other" last. Typical children also will line up cars, but they play with a car as a car, not as a thing that is blue or spins.

Obsessions/Compulsions

Repetitive behaviors also can be collections of things that people keep around themselves or actions that have to be done. A friend of mine collects rocks—not just a few, but roomfuls of rocks, particularly quartz and geodes. He says that the rocks soothe him because he understands their crystalline nature and being surrounded by their various structures gives his life a feeling of structure. Other children may fixate on one topic and try to learn everything there is to know about vacuum cleaners, and then abruptly switch to airplane schedules. Again, for a child who is high functioning, this is behavior that is similar to characteristics found among gifted children. The difference is the problem that the obsession creates: Can the child switch to another topic or is she locked into only the topic of interest, despite whether another person may or may not be interested?

Stimming

Short for "self-stimulating," stimming is when a child fixates on a repeated action, deriving great enjoyment and a feeling of peace from the action. It can be rocking, spinning, flapping, bouncing a ball, masturbating, closing a door, hitting his head, pulling on jump ropes, repeating a phrase . . . anything that is repetitive, sensorial, and reduces anxiety for the child. The difference between stimming and self-soothing behaviors is small—most people will jiggle pencils, twitch their feet, or fidget with their fingers. But when children are stimming, they often are oblivious to anything else around them and it serves to cut them off from social interaction, rather than allow them to engage in it. On one very bad day, my son locked into a phrase of "Bad Daddy" when he and my husband had locked horns and he was being sent to time out. Ray threw a 3-hour tantrum, repeating "Bad Daddy" for most of it. It was truly fearful to see him so completely out of control of his own mental state and to be using the phrase to express his anger, frustration, and fear of his own reaction.

Tito Mukhopadhyay (2000) at the age of 8, wrote that he spun because he felt that his body was a series of disconnected parts. He would see his hand and feel no sense of connection between that and his foot. He spun because he had seen that the fan blades, which were disconnected parts, would form a whole circle when they spun. He felt through the sensation of spinning that he could truly feel his body as a whole. On the other hand, Amanda, sharing her experiences via YouTube, noted that stimming is how she interacts with the world; how she gets to feel connected to and learn about the world directly without the need for language to intervene. Clearly, stimming is a significant need for children with autism and relates to their jangled neurology.

OTHER CHARACTERISTICS, NOT PART OF THE CRITERIA

There are a whole host of other issues that many children on the autism spectrum seem to experience. There is limited research data on many of these issues, and so they are not part of the diagnosis process. Hard science professionals express doubt that they even exist in the terms that experienced practitioners have created. I found that many of these issues were ones that I noticed about Elizabeth and many other mothers I knew saw them too. These are issues that directly affect your daily living and can offer strategies about dealing with the stress of autism that the parent and the child both face. It's hard for me to describe what "limited social skills" looks like, but boy, her tantrums about sand—that I could see and describe!

Sensory Integration

Many children with various forms of autism experience sensory issues—either reacting too little or too much to different stimuli. And each child is highly individual about what it is that he or she reacts to. The list of behaviors can range from odd to very odd. Tina, a friend of mine, shared a few such behaviors exhibited by her child: licking glass, licking the salt shaker, leaping out of the shopping cart to touch the carpeted pillars, chewing fingernails until they bled, spinning in circles, walking in a pattern, crying when the car stopped at red lights, screeching suddenly, having a sensitivity to light, needing to have the volume at a specific level. The list goes on and on.

Rachel's Story

Did you ever take notice of *The Incredibles* DVD main menu? Probably not . . . Ben insisted that when the colors flash red, then blue, then purple, and back to red, that we only hit start when the screen flashed purple. All hell would break loose if we did not. If we missed it, we would just wait another round of the colored backgrounds and be ready for purple. Control freak? Maybe to some, but who knows how much this affected him. His all out tantrum seemed to indicate that it was very important for the movie to start when he needed it to start. Maybe it is compensation for feeling so out of control of so many factors and gaining extreme control of a few things that helps keep him from spinning out of control.

The Sensory Processing Disorder (SPD) Foundation (2009), which specializes in research into and treatment of SPD, provides a definition:

Sensory processing (sometimes called "sensory integration" or SI) is a term that refers to the way the nervous system receives messages from the senses and turns them into appropriate motor and behavioral responses . . . *Sensory Processing Disorder* (SPD, formerly known as "sensory integration dysfunction") is a condition that exists when sensory signals *don't* get organized into appropriate responses. . . . . A person with SPD finds it difficult to process and act upon information received through the senses, which creates challenges in performing countless everyday tasks.

Motor clumsiness, behavioral problems, anxiety, depression, school failure, and other impacts may result if the disorder is not treated effectively. (para. 2–3)

For most people, this process is automatic. We hear someone talking to us, our brains receive that input and recognize it as a voice talking in a normal tone, and we respond appropriately. Children who have SPD, however, don't experience such interactions in the same way. SPD affects the way their brains interpret the information that comes in; it also affects how they respond to that information with emotional, motor, and other reactions. For example, some children are overresponsive to sensation and feel as if they're being constantly bombarded with sensory information. They may try to eliminate or minimize this perceived sensory overload by avoiding being touched or being particular about clothing. Some children are underresponsive and have an almost insatiable desire for sensory stimulation. They may seek out constant stimulation by taking part in extreme activities, playing music loudly, or moving constantly. They sometimes don't notice pain or objects that are too hot or cold, and may need high intensity input to get involved in activities. Still others have trouble distinguishing between different types of sensory stimulation.

One of the challenges of a child with high-functioning autism is that receptivity and awareness of fine sensory details is characteristic of giftedness as well. Polish psychologist Kazimierz Dabrowski (1964) noted that gifted children often expressed what he called *overexcitabilities*. The five overexcitabilities he discussed were psychomotor, sensual, emotional, intellectual, and imaginational. Gifted children often are highly responsive to sensory input as well, a very related and hard to distinguish issue from sensory integration issues. Such issues can be problematic and leads to an overrepresentation of gifted children who have SPD, according to the SPD Foundation (2009).

When I teach students about SPD, or Sensory Integration Disorder (a term first used by A. Jean Ayres in 1979), I teach them that there are actually seven senses that children with SI often cannot integrate with a sense of comfort. There are the traditional five (sight, taste, touch, smell, and hearing) and two others that researchers define as vestibular and proprioceptive.

Vestibular relates to the child's sense of balance and resides in the inner ear. According to Dr. Kern and associates from the University of Texas Southwestern Medical Center at Dallas (2007), many children on the spectrum have either an excellent or a terrible sense of balance; they tend to the extreme. I have noticed that many children with autism do not get dizzy. They have an underresponsive vestibular system. As a result, spinning tends to calm them down and they love to swing and spin for great periods of time. We went to the park two to three times a day only to swing.

Proprioceptive sense is the child's awareness of where she is in space—information received by her body and its relationship to itself. A classic study by Drs. Masterson and Biederman in 1983 found that children with autism have to rely on their sense of being touched firmly to learn new tasks rather than their visual sense. This can translate into either clumsiness or complete body awareness through focused awareness. Many children will "toe walk" or walk on their tiptoes and have an ungainly gait in which they are stiff-legged and seem as if they are barely standing upright. They may try to squeeze themselves into spaces too small for their bodies. They may not conform their body when being hugged or held. They also can have significant issues with stamina.

Elizabeth has superior proprioceptive sense—she almost never fell as a baby and walked at 9 months. I don't know if it's a feature of her autism or her own abilities, but Elizabeth is a natural athlete and has always known where she is in space. Selected for competitive gymnastics training and competing with swimmers 4 years older than she is, athletics is her area of strength and social activity. However, she is limited in her stamina. Her swimming coach says that she's a sprinter, as six laps in the pool leaves her exhausted for the rest of the day. I have very clear memories of being at a mother's group when she was 11 months old. The others were standing around chatting and snuggling their children in their arms, and I was the only mother monitoring her child as she climbed unaided up the 6-foot slide. It was not the first time I decided that mother's groups were just not for us.

Elizabeth loved baths; to this day, swimming is how she destresses. She finds her bliss moving through water, and it calms her down almost immediately. Even as a tiny baby, she loved the feeling of water. Because I was a dutiful mother of my first born, I did not use any bubble baths or water treatments to protect her soft baby skin—just like the baby manuals said. However, one evening when she was a little over a year old, our regular babysitter was more interested in entertaining her, and poured in bubble bath while Elizabeth was sitting in the tub. When I came home, they were both in tears. Elizabeth had had a tantrum and hysteria for well over an hour, and poor "Nanny Vene" had no idea what she had done to turn a sweet, happy splashing baby into a wailing banshee. It took some time (and other baths with soap bubbles) before we realized what was the cause. She completely flipped out at seeing rainbows in the water. Bubbles at parties? Not for my child!

Sand on her feet? Oh no . . . Rubbing her back? Only if you wanted to irritate her. Touch and visual things that moved and varied made her extremely agitated. But taste? She was understimulated in the area of taste. Her first food that she did not reject was spicy taco meat. She loves salty, spicy things. She dives right into pickled beets and Indian food. She is the only 8-year-old I know who likes raw green onion bulbs—banned from me since I can't stand the smell. She is a very adventurous eater and has been open to trying most new foods.

Synesthesia

Some children and parents report that the sensory information process is so confused that the information appears to get "crossed." Some researchers have hypothesized that all children are born with developing sensory neurons and as they obtain experiences, the neurological linkages "harden" and blue becomes "blue," rather than "tart." However, some people with the genetic tendency will have crossed neurons so that they then taste "tart" in their mouths when they see something blue. Not all people with synesthesia have autism, but there does appear to be a link. In his book, *Born on a Blue Day*, Daniel Tammet (2006), who has autism, states that to him colors have taste, numbers have shapes, and days have colors. The information is processed in ways that do not make sense to people with typical neurological development.

It often is the sensory issues that are the first sign that something's different . . . and it's often the one that gets noticed and remarked upon the most. As parents of our first child and adults who had limited experiences with children, we truly started noticing differences on the playground. It was watching the other children where I really began to see that perhaps Elizabeth really was different. When I read the "The Mother at the Swings" essay by Vicki Forman, I could so relate to her feelings of being alone on a crowded playground (the full essay can be found at http://www.literarymama.com/columns/specialneedsmama/archives/2006/12/the_mother_at_t.html):

The mother next to me smiles herself and says, "Boy, he really loves that, doesn't he? I mean, kids just love to swing, don't they?"

Yes, I think, *kids do love to swing*. But the reason my son loves to swing isn't the same reason her daughter, in the swing next to us, loves to swing. My son loves to swing . . . because he has what is termed "sensory integration dysfunction" and requires enhanced "vestibular input." Swinging gives my son the kind of stimulation other kids, those who can see and talk and run and ride a bike, get by simply being and doing.

. . .

The mother at the swings would like for me to tell her what it's like, how my son is different, and how he is the same. . . .

She'd like to ask, *What does his future look like?* And *How are you with all this?*

She wants to know but she doesn't know how to ask. And so she tells me that all kids love to swing.

It has taken me years to know what to say to the mother at the swings, and how to say it. To reveal the truth, graciously. . . . To tell her that yes, all children love to swing, and my son loves to swing and the reasons are both the same and different. That it's hard to watch her daughter, with her indelible eye contact and winning smile, and not mourn for what my son can't do. That some days my grief over my son is stronger than my love.

It has taken me even longer to appreciate the mother at the swings, to know that she and I have more in common than I once thought. To know that her curiosity is a mother's curiosity, one borne out of love and tenderness and a desire to understand a child, my son, one who happens to be different. That she will listen and sympathize when I offer my observations. That her compassion and thoughtfulness mean she will take the knowledge I share and use it to understand other mothers like myself, some of whom could be her neighbor, her cousin, her sister, her friend. And, finally, that she wants to know so that she can teach her own child, who also loves to swing, how to embrace and treasure what makes us all different. And the same. (Forman, 2006, para. 1, 2, 12–15)

Visual Learners

With their difficulty with social cues and language, children on the spectrum often learn best visually. In fact, Temple Grandin (2006b), who has both high-functioning autism and her Ph.D., has a book called *Thinking in Pictures*. When a child is a visual learner, it means that one must use pictures, rather than words, to better convey concepts and ideas. Some forms of technology have capitalized on this. In one particular system, called the Picture Exchange Communication System (PECS) teachers and parents present choices and information to children using pictures rather than written words. Similarly, teachers have been using visual reminders for years for children with autism (e.g., picture schedules, lunch choices, etc.).

There can be some very interesting skills that emerge from this learning ability. Some people, such as my daughter, are very spatial and have a phenomenal ability to read maps or to understand directions. At the age of 2, we were running errands before we went to the beach. My husband, who does not have a strong sense of direction, was in the righthand turn lane coming out of the bookstore. Elizabeth started screeching, "Bee . . . Bee" and frantically gesturing to the left. I turned to her, thinking she had been stung, and realized that she was trying to tell him to turn left rather than right to go to the beach. At the next intersection, I asked her which way to go and she, with a wide grin on her face, pointed in the correct direction. To this day, when my husband has to run errands, he takes Elizabeth with him.

Our house is decorated with maps. We do not live near family and so we often travel around the country to see them. The stress and anxiety of traveling with two young children with high levels of sensitivity is reduced when we can show them on the map where we are and where we're going. It helps reduce anxiety because they can relate to and understand a map. Similarly, many parents with children on the spectrum note that their children understand graphs and charts very well. They like having data nicely organized in such a visual manner.

Puzzles are another popular item among families with autism. Children with autism *love* the repetitive nature of puzzles, the visual "fit" that happens, and the problem-solving process of seeing how things fit together. Sudoku, wooden puzzles, or hidden picture puzzles all are visual games attractive to children with autism. A recent game called Qwirkle is a favorite at our house because of the visual skills needed. My daughter wins often.

These are children who must watch in order to learn. They cannot be told how to do something; they have to either do it themselves or watch others first. I often think that traditional instruction is like Charlie Brown's teacher to them—babble in a sea of noise. They tend to thrive on lists and very specific, written-down directions.

Reading can be a challenging experience for children who are very visual. Learning to read often can be very difficult because making the language connection between the visual representation of the words, the meaning of the word, and the sound of the word are three different tasks that require a great deal of mental connections. Repeated reading, where a story is read again and again, and making reading a visual task both have been found to be effective in helping these children learn to read (Bellon & Ogletree, 2000; Fossett, 2002). Yet, if children with high-functioning autism can learn to read, they often become fantastic at it. In my family, we think in visual words, not sounds. I have many words that I can use, I can write, and I can spell because I've seen them, but I can't pronounce them because that's not a visual skill.

Face-Blindness

There is one notable exception to this skill—the ability to recognize and respond to faces. Faces are certainly visual locations for information, but there is something in the emotional impact of a face that can sometimes render it almost blind to a child on the spectrum. Persons with face-blindness (or prosopagnosia) simply cannot connect faces with names or faces with particular emotions. This is not unique to autism, as many people with autism do not have it and many people with face-blindness do not have autism (however, they are issues that often occur together). In a fascinating article, Olga Bogdashina (2002) described one man's method to recognize people by their jeans, gait, movements, and hair. He can see a pattern in hair texture and process hairlines. Interestingly, many autistic children are fascinated by people's hair, and many do not recognize their relatives if they wear unfamiliar clothes. People with this disorder

Elizabeth's Friends

Age 7

Figure 4. Elizabeth's friends.

can notice small details about a face, such as hairline, scars, and other features that do not really change over time. However, the ever-changing expressions blur the understanding and ability to process their information. It is a condition that my family has to a mild degree and we have learned the fine art of having extended conversations with people when we have no idea who they are or what their name is. Recently, Elizabeth was asked to draw pictures of and describe her friends. She drew a picture of her friend Morgan (see Figure 4, Morgan is the child in the center of the top row). She completely captured Morgan's ruffles on her pink shirt, smooth red hair with a slight flip at the ends, the intricate design on her jeans, and even the untied shoes Morgan is famous for. But, she did not draw Morgan's face. Just a circle and dots for eyes. No face and no color for eyes. To Elizabeth, Morgan's face wasn't a feature that was important.

Discrepant Academic Abilities

Often, these various learning capabilities create a very uneven learning pattern. Children with high-functioning autism may excel at subjects and instruction that focus on rote memory, analysis, and visual awareness, and do poorly in areas that are highly language or socially based. They may excel at drama, but perform poorly in literature. Much of their learning will be highly dependent upon the content, their level of interest, and the method of instruction. But they may look very much like other twice-exceptional children who have significant strengths in some academic areas and very poor skills in others.

Such diverse skills found within a child with high-functioning autism can translate to test scores and cognitive abilities that are highly discrepant. For example, my daughter has a visual processing ability that is in the 95th percentile, but an auditory processing speed that is in the 9th percentile. Such wide fluctuations of scores can serve to flatten a child's overall ability or achievement scores. For example, a very bright child I worked with had an overall IQ score of 126, but a verbal score of 112 and a performance score of 135. Within each of these larger domains, he had equally wildly fluctuating subtest scores. He did not qualify for gifted services in that particular state because his overall score was not high enough, nor did he qualify for special education services because his scores were not low enough. However, many of his individual scores indicated significant strengths and some debilitating challenges. Overall, his achievement was moderate and he made grade-level B's with an occasional A.

Interestingly, according to Dawn Huber-Kinslow (2008) from The University of Iowa, prevalence rates of autism are higher among gifted populations and many gifted children are misdiagnosed or overdiagnosed with autism and other labels, because of, or exacerbated by their gifted-ness. I would recommend the book *Misdiagnosis and Dual Diagnoses of Gifted Children and Adults* by Dr. Jim Webb and others (2005) as an excellent resource for looking at children with high-functioning autism and other labels.

Physical Issues

There are few significant physical features of autism. Unlike Down syndrome, where children have very distinctive facial features and physical issues, children with autism have wide-ranging lists of physical characteristics. According to the National Human Genome Research Institute (2009), about 30% of children with autism demonstrate mild physical differences, and those who do tend to reflect slightly altered features and small head circumference.

Other issues are not fully supported by hard science, but have significant amounts of anecdotal data. As in all aspects of autism, you will need to do further research because the arguments for and against various causations and treatments tend to be very loud and controversial. Many of the physical issues of autism tend to focus on either digestive and autoimmune issues, or neurological issues such as epilepsy, seizures, or neurotransmitters.

Digestive Issues

Many children with autism can experience a variety of digestive problems, including constipation, diarrhea, acid reflux, or increased severity of autistic symptoms when eating certain foods. It is clear that children with autism often are highly selective or picky eaters. They will have lowered levels of necessary vitamins and minerals because of their restricted diets. In fact, selective eating used to be a criterion for diagnosis of autism until recently. Some researchers have reportedly found heightened levels of yeast, free radicals, auto-antibodies, or heavy metals in the blood. Other reports indicate lower levels of sulfates. These problems can result in irritable bowel syndrome, colitis, or allergies to milk, wheat, or sugar. There are some suggestions that the lack of necessary bacteria in the digestive tract can trigger an autoimmune reaction to environmental factors in some children that then becomes a biological basis for autistic behaviors. Some physical characteristics of digestive allergies and imbalances include skin dryness, dark circles, eczema, and sensitivity to light. Several projects undertaken by the University of California, Davis' M.I.N.D. Institute (n.d.) currently are examining the relationships between genetic structures, environmental toxins and triggers, and resultant types of autism. Truly, autism research is on the cutting edge of technology.

Neurological

There is a strong link between autism and epilepsy or seizures. Some estimates suggest that up to 30% of children with autism also have regular seizures. Most children with autism do not have grand mal seizures, but rather "silent," or petit mal seizures that may simply look like inattention. Daniel Tammet (2006) noted that his synesthesia, or mixing up of sensory information, began when he started having severe epilepsy seizures. Like autism, epilepsy is essentially a genetic issue, but it is a combination of multiple genes that appear to be triggered by environmental events.

There also is an interesting linkage with elevated serotonin levels in the blood of people with autism. Serotonin is strongly linked with depression, alcoholism, and anxiety, and researchers at Vanderbilt University Medical Center (Tranguch & Marino, 2008) and other medical communities are examining the role of specific proteins called serotonin transporters (SERT) that regulate the amount of serotonin available to the brain. There appears to be an issue with the serotonin transporters that regulate the serotonin created in the gut, which leads nicely back to the digestive issues often reported in children with autism. However, medications that work on the serotonin transporters don't seem to work to reduce the repetitive behaviors of children with autism.

The medical, physical, and neurological complexities of autism are fascinating to study, but they are a tangled web of confusing and often contradictory information. Much of the research is being conducted currently, and I do not feel entirely comfortable as a layperson describing the intricacies of various proteins and their interactions. I encourage you to stay tuned as our knowledge base continues to grow rapidly in this area.

I do know that anxiety, depression, and alcoholism run rampant in both my family and that of my husband. I do know that we read the checklists of autism when we were first looking for help, and read of characteristics that we had learned to live with and even celebrate, within ourselves and family members. I do know that we often find ourselves staring into an abyss of confusion, guilt, and worry. And I also know that we love our children more than I can comprehend, and we celebrate the special things that make them *who* they are, that go beyond physical, social, and language issues. My children are perfect. I just needed to know the best ways to help them become the best that they can be.

DESCRIBING MY CHILD

The problem with checklists and descriptors is that they still don't capture the wonderful, funny essence of any child, much less mine. I read so many checklists and realized that Elizabeth fit many of them. I kept holding their descriptions up against Elizabeth, much like shopping for clothes—Does *this* label fit her? How about this one? Untangling autism from the essential "Elizabeth-ness" sometimes can be problematic. Does she have communication problems, or is she just that way? Does she have significant sensitivities, or is she just a member of our family (who all hate loud noises and like nuts in our ice cream because of the texture)? And what about her strengths? Were these autism at its best or a version of giftedness? She has a very strong spatial ability, phenomenal abilities with puzzles, and unbelievable athletic skills—how could such strengths be characteristic of a terrible label such as autism? And all mothers deal with tantrums; my mother was full of stories of my crankiness and my severe inability to fall asleep and I turned out fine . . . didn't I?

And did she really fit the label? Yes, she had some characteristics, but not all. Was I being paranoid? She was a *girl*—girls weren't supposed to have autism. Here was a child who loved kisses, smiled at me, and made funny faces at herself in the mirror. She reminded me of the nursery rhyme:

There was a little girl
Who had a little curl
Right in the middle of her forehead
And when she was good

She was very, very good
And when she was bad, she was horrid.

And I didn't want a label; a label might provide my child with that very future that I was trying to avoid—the ones that so many other mothers on blogs and bulletin boards were living full of pain and hope for their beloved child, and who do not measure their progress against other children, but only against themselves. Mothers who celebrated a child's first sentence at age 7. Families who could not travel on airplanes because of the extreme meltdowns. Was I one of *those* mothers? Or was I a mother who was simply unprepared for motherhood? But we did need help. And so finally we went looking . . .

I Don't Think We're in Kansas Anymore, Toto: Diagnosis

MAKING IT REAL—TOO REAL

Getting a diagnosis is absolutely critical to getting help. There is no help available for children with high levels of abilities, so it is critical that a diagnosis of a disability be made. A 2009 study by Dr. Paul Shattuck and colleagues at Washington University of St. Louis found that most children on the spectrum are not officially diagnosed until they are 6 years old, quite late to receive the critical intervention services they need to improve. But some help is better than no help. In today's world, no label means no services. Insurance companies—for those of you with insurance companies who do anything—Early Intervention programs, schools, therapists—*all* require a diagnosis. You cannot get treatment or help without a diagnosis. It is truly the ticket to help.

But oh, what a ticket it is. We spent Elizabeth's second birthday at a speech therapist's office. I had called a friend of mine in Colorado who knew someone in Florida, so we trekked the 6 hours to Jacksonville to meet with Judy, who was truly doing us a favor. No one would even take my calls until Elizabeth was 2, and I was told at every corner that they would not even put us on the waiting list for evaluation until she was 2. The waiting lists were 2–3 months long—just for diagnosis! I was also told that treatment waiting lists were even longer, but I couldn't even get on those lists until I got a diagnosis. I called Early Intervention and private speech therapists. After being told it was $150–$250 an hour just for diagnosis purposes, but *free* if I went through our state's Early Intervention program, I knew that Early Intervention was the way to go. Judy was charging us only $100 for our visit, and I figured that it was worth it: I could get a diagnosis, get on lists, and start the ball rolling. What I really wanted was to be told was that it was all in my head: I was a bad mommy and my daughter really was fine. Nothing a little change in parenting couldn't fix. I wanted to be told I could fix it.

Judy was very nice and I was amused, not for the first time, at how much fun speech therapy looks. She had toys all over her office and a very kid-friendly waiting room. I sat with Elizabeth as Judy played sound games with her—"What does the cow say?" "Moo! Can you say Moo?"—in a very cheery, friendly voice. However, I knew she was doomed.

To begin with, we do not live on a farm. We didn't even live near a farm. My husband grew up in Greece and is totally amused at how much farming is part of the American culture. We teach our children to say farm animal sounds although they will probably only visit a farm a few times. It's much more useful to teach them what a phone sounds like, or the sound of an airplane, or what to say when ordering pizza. Really, when was the last time you, as an adult, were asked what a chicken says? Therefore we had not taught our daughter farm animal sounds.

Plus, she never copied sounds. She would watch my mouth and could respond to directions and she could put together 50-piece puzzles, but she would not copy sounds. She could say "mama" clearly, but that's it. No, she was not going to be copying Judy's farm sounds.

Judy came back with a diagnosis of dyspraxia or "lazy tongue." My first reaction was, "Huh? And here I was worried about autism!" However, Judy did tell us that she really didn't think that Elizabeth had autism: she made eye contact, she followed directions and understood what was said to her, and she responded to laughter and her name. We left feeling rather foolish and paranoid. Such a lack of diagnosis by a variety of professionals is common for children with high-functioning autism. But I still wasn't going to give up my place on those waiting lists. Regardless of *what* the problem was, we knew we still needed help. I called up Early Intervention and was put on the waiting list for diagnosis. They were happy to look at Judy's data, but they had to do their own process. More waiting . . .

EARLY INTERVENTION

At the end of May 2003 we were finally seen by Early Intervention (EI). It is an amazing program funded through the federal government and required by law. All communities will have access to free diagnosis and therapy for kids with disabilities. The quality of the programs will vary, of course, but I have never been so thrilled as I was with our Early Intervention program.

To begin with, the EI folks came to our house *and* even made sure it was at a time when no one was going down for naps. These were people well used to working with the schedules of toddlers! I cleaned like a mad woman, of course. I was still wiping down the counters as they came in. I was *not* going to have them see the mess our house was in normally with two active and challenging toddlers. In other words, they saw a fake version of us. I knew that Ray would insist on being part of the process, so I sent him out with our babysitter for an afternoon at the park. There was a team of three people, and they got down on the floor and got out backpacks of yet more toys. They engaged her in play and cheered for her when she dragged out her puzzle to show them she could put together a map of the U.S. (I'm telling you—the kid did and still does have an amazing sense of geography.) She was showing off and loving it. No words, though. They tried gentle pressure—"Do you want Florida or Texas? Tell me." She solved the problem by grabbing Texas and putting it into place. I was pretty well convinced we had passed, which meant "failed," meaning we might get services.

I was *very* aware of time ticking. Elizabeth was now 2 years, 3 months old, and Early Intervention ended at age 3 by federal law. (That law was changed in 2004—it now ends at age 6. Too late for us, but I was *so* happy at the change in the law.) We had already been on the waiting list for diagnosis for 3 months. But no help yet. More paperwork was needed. We then had to set up a meeting to make a plan. Luckily, for my patience, that meeting was held only a few weeks later—but tick, tick, tick—Elizabeth was now 2 years, 3.5 months old.

At the meeting, they told me she definitely qualified for "developmentally delayed" and I had another moment of "huh?" They explained to me that *all* children with delays were identified this way; they didn't use labels so that the services would match the child's needs and not the child's label. Even very severe children were diagnosed with this catch-all label. They didn't use autism or dyspraxia or speech delay. All services were to be free to me, and to be as natural as possible. Wonderful! That meant that they would work with all of us: the family, her school, and her therapy. Fantastic! She qualified for speech therapy and occupational therapy. Great! And then they handed me a list of "qualified providers" (five pages worth!) and left my house. Once again, I was in waiting list hell . . .

I called every name on the list. How on Earth was I supposed to know which providers were "good" and which ones were just taking money from the government? The great irony was that I have a background in special education. I'm *supposed* to know this stuff. But I worked with public schools. I worked with teachers who are working with kids with disabilities. I knew *nothing* about how to pick a therapist. I went with the group that had the shortest waiting list; only 2 more months of waiting.

Picking a Therapist

Choosing a therapist is one of the most difficult things to do—and one of the most important. However, you cannot let the knowledge of the importance of this task freeze your decision-making abilities. Time *is* of the essence, and you can always change therapists if it isn't working out. Of course, the best ones probably have waiting lists that are lengthy, so you will have to balance your sense of urgency with the availability of who you *really* want. Remember, just because a particular therapist worked wonders for a child of a friend of yours, doesn't mean that he is the only therapist for your child. According to Howard Erman (2006), you want to look for:

- *Connection*: Someone who will work with you and who you feel has your child's best interest at heart. It doesn't necessarily have to be someone you would be friends with, just someone who is willing to work with you.

- *Recommendations*: In today's electronic world, almost all reputable therapists will have a review listing somewhere. Read the comments and do a Google search to find the comments that might not be officially sanctioned. Do recognize that one person with a grievance can raise a lot of fuss. Look for patterns in the comments.

- *Training*: Check the therapist's professional lineage. Is her graduate school well-known and is it accredited? There are an awful lot of "pseudo" higher education institutions; make sure that your therapist comes with national or state accreditation or affiliation with an organization.

- *Insight*: Look for someone who sees your child with an eye for growth and can help you perceive things in new ways as well. Therapists are there to listen to you—but you want someone you can learn from as well.

- *Experience*: Ideally, the therapist should have a decade or more of working with children like your child. That being said, our speech therapist was brand new, and she was marvelous because she knew brand-new techniques. But she was in a partnership where there were other, more experienced therapists who all collaborated together and mentored her. Generally, the more experienced therapists get better results.

- ◆ *Cost*: You do yourself and your child no good if you go into significant debt in order to pay for the therapy. Go with the best you can afford, but make sure you can afford it. Most insurance companies will have some form of coverage, and many states are now requiring insurance companies within that state to cover services for children with autism. If you are not in one of those states, or, as in our case, your insurance explicitly denies speech or occupational therapy, ask the therapist if they know of any other (legal) approaches. And remember, there is always the list of free therapists through Early Intervention.
- ◆ *Location*: You will probably be visiting a speech, behavioral, or occupational therapist a lot—two or three or even five times a week. You will want to pick someone who is close to the rest of your life—your work, your home, and the child's school or day care. If you are in a rural area, consider the inconvenience of traveling an extensive distance for each visit.

Tick, tick, tick . . . Elizabeth was almost 2 ½ years old when she finally saw a therapist's office. We spent 6 months of the one year that the system would allot us waiting for that help. And no one would let us start the process until the pediatrician gave the OK for there to *be* a problem. And the pediatrician wouldn't acknowledge any sort of problem until Elizabeth's language appeared as an item on the magic developmental checklist. Because she exhibited so many strengths, the areas of challenge were not seen as areas to be addressed until they appeared on the appropriate checklist.

Getting to Early Intervention

The biggest piece of advice I give parents who come to talk to me is "Push early, push hard!" If I had realized that there would be 6 months of waiting for help, I would have started screaming earlier. The window of language development is very tight—the earlier you start language therapy, the more effective it is. The later you wait, the longer therapy takes to work well. If you bandage a newborn kitten's eye at birth, it will be functionally blind after 3 weeks, even if you remove the bandage. Neurons have to be activated early in order to work later. If damage occurs at the wrong time and therapy does not start soon enough, there are sometimes irreversible problems.

However, the brain has a wonderful ability to be "plastic." In some cases, such as terrible car accidents where we know of specific damage to the brain, other parts of the brain can take over those functions after some time learning those functions. The brain has a remarkable ability to heal itself. It's why I'm in special education: I love the challenge of teaching a child to learn different ways "around" his problems.

It Is Never Too Late to Get Started, But the Earlier, the Better

But there are so many gatekeepers and so many layers of paperwork and bureaucracy to go through. "Early" Intervention—my ass! It should be called "Until we have time to get to you" Intervention. However, the waiting part was the *only* bad thing about them: I have never worked with a kinder, more helpful group than the professionals who showed up at my door to help me help my child.

Every state is required to have Early Intervention—it's part of federal law and is funded through a combination of state funds and federal monies. However, each state has a different process by which it's activated. They also all have different names. Some states call it Early Intervention, others "First Steps." Whatever it's called in your state, it's there and pediatricians are the gatekeepers.

All pediatricians are required to keep in contact with the state's "Child Find" program, or some variation of that name. They report everything they do from immunizations, to weight of children, to medical issues they're seeing. When your child's doctor suggests that you contact Early

Intervention, it is not a gentle suggestion like your neighbor might make—it means she is making a report to the state that you have been referred. It sounds intimidating, but it's to help make sure that parents who don't know what they're doing get appropriate help for their children as quickly as possible. Pediatricians truly are looking out for the interest of the child.

However, because doctors are the gatekeepers, they also are the ones who allow or disallow you to enter. I made the mistake of not pushing enough, and so we were locked out of help for several months. Another mother of a child who has since been diagnosed shares that

> when he was little and kept crying about everything, we spent a lot of time struggling to get him to calm down. Why was he so irritable and frustrated? I took him to his pediatrician, and was told that he was fine and that I "needed to be more firm." Thanks. When he was 3 and about to start preschool, we took him for a check-up and I mentioned the behavior issues. I was told that since he interacted with his younger brother so well, it couldn't be autism. Really?

In many of the books written by mothers of children with autism, particularly children with high-functioning autism, they each share how they changed pediatricians because they kept being told that their child was "fine" or that it was their fault. All of them were doing research on their own and no one would listen. Unfortunately, this is all too often a common story among families. Not only are you struggling to help your child, you're trying to find others to believe you.

In their defense, pediatricians have to make a judgment call, based off of limited experience with a child and only the strength of the parents' concerns. I am convinced that the standard "Oh, I'm sure its fine" is not a "diagnosis," but a "test" of the parents to determine the level of their concern. It's a trick I do with my own children now. When they fall, I do not fuss over them because that will only make them think that every fall is a big deal. I tell them they're fine. "Oh, Elizabeth, I'm sorry you fell. You're fine. Brush it off, and you can get right back up and play." If they're truly fine, they believe me and bounce right back up. If they're not, they'll continue to howl, and I know that it really is something serious. It is not, however, a good listening strategy. And when symptoms are vague and different mostly in severity from other kids, you leave your pediatrician's office convinced that you're being a worry-wart. And the worst of all—you worry that you're a whiner of a parent.

There are tools available for pediatricians and you as well. The Modified Checklist for Autism in Toddlers (M-CHAT) is available to use as early as 16 months. Although language is not a strong indicator at 16 months, there are numerous questions related to eye contact, use of pointing, communication efforts, and types of play. The Video Glossary, developed by researchers out of the University of Florida, is available online at the Autism Speaks website (see http://www.autismspeaks.org/video/glossary.php). It shows videotaped differences between a typical baby or toddler and a baby with autism asked to perform the same tasks.

LABELS ARE FOR FOOD, NOT PEOPLE

The Early Intervention folks told me that they didn't label. That sounds great in theory, but in reality I was obsessed with finding out *what* was happening to my little girl and what I could expect and what I could do. Jenny McCarthy (2006), in her wonderful book, talked about the "University of Google." Go ahead and Google "developmental delay." I got more than 2 ½ *million* sites when I did that. Needless to say, it didn't help me very much. I wanted words for what was happening. I wanted to *know*!

I spent hours that added up to days on Google. I read everything I could about dyspraxia, apraxia, echolalia, Sensory Integration Disorder . . . and every site took me deeper and deeper into despair. I knew that I had a daughter who wasn't talking. I knew that she had signs of Sensory

Integration Disorder. I kept finding that these terms related to autism. But I also knew that she exhibited characteristics of giftedness. Did she have autism? The yes/no answer became an obsession with me. I read blogs; I read bulletin boards. I did *not* post anything—probably out of fear that someone would ask me, "Why are you here? She doesn't have autism!" and worse, yet, someone might say, "Welcome to the mommy club of children with autism." I wasn't ready to commit either way. Part of me was still convinced that this was bad parenting—something I could fix with the right game, the right discipline strategy, the right . . . something, whatever that might be.

And oh, I cried. With every blog, with every posting on a bulletin board, I saw my daughter's future. I read of mothers who were celebrating their 8-year-old child's first three-word sentence. I read of children who drooled. I read of classmates teasing children. I read of children being forgotten on field trips. I read of emergency room visits from children banging their heads on walls. I read of parents who learned to let go of typical expectations and celebrate the small gains of their child. And in every blog, I tested the reality as my own: Is *this* what's going to happen to *my* child? Is *this* her future? And I cried.

During one of her speech therapy sessions, I brought up the issue of a label to the therapist. "What label do you think she'd qualify under if Early Intervention had labels?" I asked hesitantly. With great sympathy, the therapist said, "Autism, I think." I finally had it—someone who knew about it told me my daughter had autism. And no one, anywhere, mentioned that she might be gifted, too. They were so focused on their concern with her disability that they didn't know that some of her behavior might be indicative of gifted behavior as well.

We finally got an official label the week she turned 3. In the meeting where she transitioned from Early Intervention to Special Education, they informed me that she would qualify for services based on her label of autism. Now it was "real."

TOO MUCH INFORMATION

I received so many pieces of paper about disabilities. At the pediatrician's office when we got the initial referral, I got information about Early Intervention and some of the developmental delays they served. At Early Intervention, at every therapist's office, I received more information. And I found unimaginable amounts of information electronically. There are literally 19 *million* sites that come up when you search for "autism" in Google. There are days I feel as if I've read every one of them, and yet, I'll find a new one and a whole new community lives there. The amount of information on autism is beyond comprehension, and yet there is still so much to be known. I found myself in the bogs of information overload—too much to make sense of, and yet I needed to make decisions now.

One of the traits that I share with my children is that I shut down when I'm overwhelmed. I did not seek out the very support groups that I was needing because I felt myself in too much of a panic. None of my friends had a child with autism, and I didn't have anyone to hold my hand and lead me to a group. I also knew that my child did not have severe autism, and I felt guilty at crying about my child's issues when other mothers were dealing with much more significant issues. I now know how helpful a friendly voice would have been during this time and the toll it took on me, my marriage, and my friendships because I did not have a support network. But how can you take more time when you're drowning in information, decisions, and moment-to-moment experiences? And how do you find support when your child "fits" the classification, but not the label of the support group?

D-DAY: GETTING A DIAGNOSIS

One parent describes D-Day (Diagnosis Day) as equally as Earth-shattering as Birth Day—but not in a good way. Getting the diagnosis of autism for us was anticlimactic, but getting the diagnosis of developmentally delayed was . . . altering. I remember watching Elizabeth that afternoon, trying to see if she *really* was developmentally delayed, or if they had made a terrible mistake. Maybe we would all wake up from this and she would be fine and I could relax, just an overly excited first-time parent. Maybe I really was overdramatizing this whole thing. Maybe they just felt my panic. Maybe she was just some form of giftedness and I was exaggerating something good to be bad. Maybe . . . I would not have been surprised if she had grown two heads or turned into a dripping, frothing monster that afternoon. I was so afraid that the label had changed her—or changed my perception of her. Elizabeth was, and still is, perfect to me in my eyes, but my perfect dream of parenthood was gone.

SHARING THE NEW MAP

Telling other people was tricky. Understanding it *myself* was hard. I couldn't use the term "developmentally delayed" because no one knew what that term meant. Trying on the word "autism" was like picking at a scab—it hurt an awful lot if I kept at it. My husband didn't have the preconceptions that I did; he wasn't in the field of education, nor did he grow up in the United States, and to him, autism was a word he related to "self" because of his association with the Greek language. He asked me to lead the way and to keep him informed; a pattern we established where I did the research and then processed aloud with him and sought his advice. We were both deeply involved, but in different ways. He also was positive that we were headed in the right direction. Any action was better than no action. His practical and loving support helped us focus on what we could all do, rather than what she couldn't. He didn't understand autism, but he wasn't afraid of it.

But I noticed that when I told people that my daughter had autism, there was either a reaction of, "Oh, Claire, you're making a much bigger deal of this than it is," or "Oh, wow . . . autism, huh?" A common response has been, "You must be such a saint."

There is such a common perception among the general public that parents of children with disabilities are themselves somehow very special people—touched with "sainthood." The reality is, as anyone who knows me can tell you, I ain't no saint. I get frustrated, I cry, I swear on occasion, and I sulk. I'm afraid of what might happen, and I'm a tiger for my child. And don't *most* mothers feel that way? I roll my eyes at the "saint" thing because it's a way for parents of a typical child to (a) feel glad that *they* don't have to deal with challenging behaviors and (b) keep any "taint" of autism away from them. In the Greek culture, there is the concept of an "evil eye" or the idea that bad things will happen to you if you are too good or too successful. When people say that parents of children with disabilities are saints, I believe that what they are really saying is: "This could never happen to me. God only gives you what you can handle and I couldn't handle that. You, clearly, are such a good person that God gave this hard thing for you to handle. Good thing I'm not that strong!" For saints are not of this world, and most of us could never aspire to be one. It's a way of keeping the "evil eye" off of them—and it totally dehumanizes us. If we dare to complain, we must not be saintly, and are therefore not worthy of this burden we have been given. It's why I find solace in being with other mothers. We can share all of our conflicted emotions and there's no one judging us on how bad a mother we are.

I was amused to learn of a group of women who call themselves "Mothers from Hell." They have realized that they have to be their child's advocate and they are prepared to take on the world. There are organizations whose entire mission is to be advocates and to help fight for children's rights. They are having tremendous impact on laws and insurance policies. I will discuss these organizations in a later section. But far from being "saintly," these parents and advocates focus on stirring things up, changing the status quo, and making sure that other parents do not have to go through what they went through.

Telling Others

Susan Senator (2005) described how she *acts* to let others know that her child has a difference. She acts very "in charge" and speaks loudly and clearly to her son, using short words, so that everyone around her can hear that she is treating him differently because he *is* different. She indicates by her voice that her son needs more coaching than other children, but that she is well in control. She noted how she would get appreciative glances, rather than the sighs and eye rolling she had gotten previously.

She also noted that there were times, such as the lines at Disney theme parks, where they used autism to their advantage. They decided to ask for disability access, rather than subject herself and the public to the scene that was sure to happen if they had to stand in line for hours at a time. She got lots of ugly looks because her son did not physically appear to have a disability, and of course, he behaved perfectly. But she also knew that if they were to wait in lines, he would *not* be behaving perfectly. She was caught between the hypothetical and the realistic. You wonder at times when you're using autism as an excuse, not a reason.

I've had a similar experience. There was a poor mother at the park whose son wanted to swing as well. Elizabeth was pitching a fit to stay in the swing, and Ray was starting to scream as well. The mother asked me, "Can't you just hurry her up?" I lost my temper and said, "NO, I CAN'T! She has autism!" The mother gave me a look of total shock and quickly moved her son to the other side of the playground. I wanted yell at her, "He won't catch it!" but I didn't. The reality was that Elizabeth was just having a fairly typical fit by a toddler who didn't want to get off the swings. One good glare from me and a firm "When I count to three, you will get off of that swing" was all it took to stop that behavior. But I was tired and out of sorts and had been brooding and feeling sorry for myself. *Was* I using autism as an excuse? At that particular point, probably yes. But I was so tired of constantly having to monitor our movements: Was this a good time to go to the grocery store? Do I have time to run into the pharmacy before tiredness/stress/anxiety made everything difficult?

Could I take her to the speech therapist, drop her off to my husband at home, and still have time to make it to my class I had to teach?

The word autism comes laden with preconceptions. When I told teachers that Elizabeth had autism, they looked at her as though they expect her to start rocking violently and banging her head against the wall. I have now learned to introduce Elizabeth to schools by telling them that she has "speech delays and some sensory challenges." Then, after they've gotten to know her, I can use the word autism.

Telling our friends was a bit anticlimactic. Many of them said, "Well, hadn't you suspected?" I found myself initially hurt that they didn't understand the trauma that came from having someone confirm my suspicions. None of them had had a child with a disability, and so my experience was new for them as well. But then, as now, I found myself struck at how they never placed expectations on me or my daughter. I soon learned which friends were real "rocks" with whom I could have catch-up conversations after months of being in research hell and who drifted away over time. I read where it was important to educate your old support network about autism in addition to finding a new support network. I didn't really have time to keep my friends in the loop (it was hard enough keeping my husband and family), but the ones that truly knew me just seemed to accept Elizabeth's differences as they accepted my quirks, and we moved on together.

Telling our family was another challenge. My mother immediately started seeking out brain treatments and sending me information to read. She listened to me and cried with me and encouraged me to stop feeling sorry for myself and go do something. She also reminded me that Elizabeth was still Elizabeth. Getting a label did not change my child and my job was the job of any mother: helping my child be the very best she could be. A label simply gave me access to more help. She has never seen Elizabeth or Ray in anything other than a positive light or a puzzle to be solved.

My husband's family was a bit different. His aunts sent to Jerusalem for a special silver icon and traveled to Cyprus to have it blessed by the bishop there. They told us that they were so sad and that they prayed constantly for her to get better. In my anger and frustration one day, I yelled at my husband, "It's not like she has CANCER, for God's sake! She's only autistic! It's not like she's going to DIE! We just have to DEAL with it, not FIX her!" Other friends of mine have had their mothers blame them—"It's not really autism, you're just spoiling that child"—or blame their husbands—"You should never have married him." Reactions can vary widely, needless to say. Autism is so misunderstood and so confusing, that we and our families often don't know how to react.

I'm only now telling Elizabeth and Ray. My mother was deeply concerned that telling them would imply that I see them as anything less than perfect, and that children need to know that their parents love them unconditionally. I completely and totally love my children, but I also know that they have struggled and will continue to struggle and that I need to give them tools to handle their own issues. Dawn Huber-Kinslow (2008) stressed that it is important to tell your children early, in age-appropriate words, and with visual supports. Knowledge is power, and I will not have them blaming themselves. When I told Elizabeth, Ray, in unending sibling rivalry, immediately wanted to know what he had, too. It's an interesting feeling telling your children that they both have labels. In Ray's case, he has Tourette's syndrome and anxiety disorder. He appeared pleased by the fact that his sister wasn't the only one who had a label, but didn't appear overly curious. He's only 7, so we're going to talk about it as it comes up.

However, Elizabeth is 8, with a label that is going to get more public reaction than anxiety disorder. I got her permission to write this book, which she is convinced will make her famous. However, in getting her permission, I told her that she had a medical condition called autism that makes it harder for her to find words or talk with people, and that sometimes she feels things more than other people. Telling a child she is different is tricky, particularly for a preteen girl in today's society. I know that her knowledge of herself as different is going to shape her perception of herself as a teenager, as a woman, and as a person. Eventually, I will expose her to the wonderful books that have been written by people with autism that can capture the experience better than I can. If I think it will help, I will introduce her to the online support communities of people with autism. I have purposefully taken the route of "medical difference" to let her know that *she* did not cause this, she has to manage it her whole life, and that while autism may be a reason, it is never an excuse. For her, I am trying to explain autism like asthma—asthma doesn't have to stop you from being a professional athlete, you just have to manage it. Autism won't stop her from doing anything she wants to—she just has to learn to manage it and even to use its characteristics to her advantage. Autism can be a gift, but it takes a lot of unwrapping.

I have learned since that there are several things you can do when the shock of diagnosis hits you. These include:

- *Taking time to process*: Grieve the way you need to, but do not isolate yourself.
- *Finding books and blogs written by other mothers of children with autism*: In the Resources section, I list a number of them; they each had a different voice and something I could learn from. I felt like I was reading *my* story and their strength gave me strength. They understood my hurt at the imperfect world that we have to deal with.
- *Talking to a therapist who has experience with families with disabilities*: The Early Intervention folks will probably know someone to recommend. Men often handle the shock of diagnosis differently than mothers do. They can find support at The Fathers Network at http://www.fathersnetwork.org.
- *Knowing that you have the power to share when and what you want*: Not everyone around you needs to know everything.

- *Realizing that autism has become so common these days that it does not have the stigma that it used to*: The more you share with people, the more likely you'll find others with a story also.
- *Keeping your appointments*: Get your hair cut, go to lunch, get the car washed. Make sure your life rhythms stay as close to how they were before the diagnosis as possible.

There is a column by Erma Bombeck that has helped many, many mothers. A friend of mine has it framed in her bathroom. You can find the whole piece at http://www.child-autism-parent-cafe.com/some-mothers-chosen-by-god.html (I've quoted part of it here for you).

Some Mothers Chosen By God

Most women become mothers by accident, some by choice, a few by social pressures and a couple by habit.

This year, nearly 100,000 women will become mothers of handicapped children.

Did you ever wonder how mothers of handicapped children are chosen? . . . He passes a name to an angel and smiles, "Give her a handicapped child."

The angel is curious. "Why this one, God? She's so happy."

"Exactly," smiles God. "Could I give a handicapped child a mother who does not know laughter? That would be cruel."

"But has she patience?" asks the angel.

"I don't want her to have too much patience or she will drown in a sea of self-pity and despair. . . . I watched her today. She has that feeling of self and independence that is so rare and so necessary in a mother. You see, the child I'm going to give her has his own world and that's not going to be easy."

"But Lord, I don't think she even believes in you."

God smiles. "No matter. I can fix that. This one is perfect. She has just enough selfishness."

The angel gasps, "Selfishness? Is that a virtue?"

God nods. "If she can't separate herself from the child occasionally, she'll never survive. Yes, here is a woman whom I will bless with a child who is less than perfect. She doesn't realize it yet, but she is to be envied. She will never take for granted a 'spoken word.' She will never consider a 'step' ordinary. . .

"I will permit her to see clearly the things I see... ignorance, cruelty, prejudice... and allow her to rise above them. She will never be alone. I will be at her side every minute of every day of her life because she is doing my work as surely as she is here by my side." (Bombeck, 1983)

TRAVELING "WITH" OR "TRAVELER"?

Autism is almost tangible at times. When Elizabeth is particularly stressed or tired, I can almost see the fibers of autism cloud her ability to react, find words, and handle information coming at her. It directly impacts her ability to access her strengths, particularly her analytical ability. When she's in a social situation or in a new place, she gets a "little girl lost" expression in her eyes that breaks my heart. I can sense her searching for the right word, the right behavior. She'll watch people intensely, trying to figure out the "code." Even in happy times, I can sometimes see autism slide its tendrils around her reactions. I have a photograph of her right after she scored a goal in soccer. She's windmilling her arms, and her tongue is out. I know her well enough to know that is her form of stimming and experiencing things with her tongue. Even in joy, the autism sings its siren call that shuts off language from her: "Right here, right now . . . don't think, just feeeeeel!"

In her powerful video essay, "In My Language," on YouTube, Amanda Baggs (2007) noted that it is only when she interacts with the right things in the right way that she is considered to have thought. When she interacts, feels, tastes, or smells the wrong things in the wrong way, she is considered to be in a world of her own, rather than people understanding that she is experiencing the world in a different way. In a computer-aided voiceover, she noted that there was no meaning to her flickering her hand through the water in her video, no ulterior purpose—she was just engaged with the water, watching its flickering patterns, not searching for its relationship to anything else. She was merely interacting with the water as it interacted with her. She observed that she is considered to be limited when really it is others who are limited in their understanding of her. The piece is even more impactful when you know that the voiceover is provided by the computer voice "reading" the words she is typing. Amanda does not directly talk to the audience, but allows us insight into her mind through modern technology. She is, indeed, human—but a human who perceives things that many of us do not. It is a tempting world of experience . . .

However, at least in our family, autism separates Elizabeth, and those family members with similar characteristics from others—and from themselves. There is a strong temptation to interact with objects, words, and things that disconnect you from powerful emotions. In her book, Patricia Stacey (2003) noted that her son, rather than not feeling, would feel *too* strongly, and that autism allowed him to escape the pain of those powerful emotions. He would retreat into his "safe place" where he would not be scared, anxious, or distraught. Even powerful positive emotions would send him retreating by the very force of their impact. Even Temple Grandin (2006a, 2006b) in her amazing autobiographical explanations of autism has stated that she craved a feeling of safety that her "squeeze machine" could provide.

There is an intense debate within the field of autism about whether you should use the terms "people with autism" or "autistic people." Called "people-first language," the phrase "people with autism" emphasizes the humanity of the person first and his area of disability second. People with autism are not defined in their personhood by their disability; it just happens to be a characteristic that they have. But in a powerful essay "Why I Dislike Person-First Language," Jim Sinclair (1999) stated that he *is* autistic, just as he is generous. You would never say a "person with generosity." He also noted that placing autism last implies that is something that can be separated from the person, like a coat. He notes that his autism shapes who he is—part of his personality—it is him and he is autism.

I am torn by this. There is a powerful statement also by Jim Sinclair in his 1993 essay "Don't Mourn for Us" in which he said, "This is what we know, when you tell us of your fondest hopes and dreams for us: that your greatest wish is that one day we will cease to be, and strangers you can love will move in behind our faces" (para. 9). Similarly, there is a very sad story of Karen McCarron, a mother from Illinois, who smothered Katie, her 3-year-old daughter. According to a *USA Today* article (Mercer, 2008), when asked why she did this, Karen responded, "Maybe I could fix her this way, and in heaven she would be complete" (para. 3). Of course such stories are horrific beyond belief, but I can understand that aspect of hating autism and what it does to my child. I love my daughter and like any parent, I struggle to know and support who she IS, not who I want her to be. Is autism part of who she is, or is it something that is separate from her and impacts her, much like a chronic disease? We happily claim her gifts as part of who she is. Why not her challenges? I can't tell you the absolute answer, but I do believe that it is both to some degree—it has shaped her personality and I constantly struggle with keeping her "in the world" where she feels safe enough to deal with new situations and new stimuli. I work on teaching her coping strategies and words for things she is afraid of and does not know how to explain, and I work on helping her to observe herself and others. I work on keeping her engaged with this world and away from the seductive world of languagelessness where she feels no pain or fear.

THE TRIP YOU WERE "SUPPOSED" TO HAVE: OUGHTISM

My daughter has 75 baby dolls all named Lily. Actually, they're not truly named Lily. She was carrying one once when I was taking my children through the lobby of the hotel at a conference I was attending. Someone I knew stopped me to say "Hello" and kindly leaned down to ask Elizabeth, "What's the name of your baby?" Elizabeth learned long ago to mumble a noncommittal "Lalable" when she can't think of what to say. "Lily? Oh that's a nice name!" replied my acquaintance. Elizabeth nodded enthusiastically and said "Lily" the next time someone asked her what her baby's name was. Of course, it was a different baby doll . . .

Elizabeth loved baby dolls. Not necessarily because they *were* babies, but because other little girls had them. She didn't dress them, didn't change them, didn't wrap them up—just carried them and that made her happy. She also loved pushing them in a stroller. Not pretending, just pushing. Sometimes, she carried two of them. None of them appeared to be a particular favorite. But when asked 5 years in a row, "What do you want for Christmas?" she would always answer, "Baby dolls!"

I was particularly saddened by this. I *loved* dolls myself, and I have very distinct memories of playing for hours with my dolls. There's a family story of how I would carry dirt clods around and say that they were my "babies." But each of my dolls had her own particular name and personality, and I would have elaborate games and stories surrounding the dolls. I know that it is this love of dolls that turned into a love of children that led me to teaching. I had saved some of my dolls for my daughter, who "some day" would love them, too. They still sit in storage because I could not bear to have "Wendy," "Anastasia," and "Julie" join the legion of nameless babies sitting in my daughter's toy chest. They sit, waiting for my child to understand the importance of names.

Presents

Finding presents for a child on the spectrum can be difficult. You're in a quandary of "Do I get him a toy that he *wants*, or a toy that he *needs*?" Choosing age-appropriate toys is not always right; these children may have no interest in dolls, games, or bikes. Yet, you're afraid that getting your child what she really wants will either (a) aggravate the autism that you're fighting against, or (b) add to the growing collection of obsessive items. Did Elizabeth *really* need one more baby doll to add to the 75 she already has? But she didn't want baby doll clothes, Barbies, or doll houses. She only wanted to carry around the baby doll. As a friend of mine says, "We're trying to get him to play imaginatively. Do I *want* him to have blocks that he will just line up obsessively?" Plus, as one mother whose blog I read noted, buying Elmo for an 8-year-old just reminded her of how different her child really was. She bought it for him, but with tears.

Yet, on the other hand, buying them age-appropriate toys can have a two-fold purpose. First, they provide the raw materials for teaching the child more age-appropriate play strategies. My daughter had no idea what to do with baby dolls. However, she carefully watched other girls and decided that they were for carrying. Parents tell stories about playing with trucks and playdough, and modeling play activities for their children. Secondly, great toys can be an inducement for other children to come over to your house to play. We bought Elizabeth beautiful "dress-up" clothes, not because she necessarily enjoyed them, but because our house would be a treasure trove for the neighborhood children. Nicole was a little girl 2 years younger than Elizabeth who would come over every day to play in Elizabeth's treasure trunk. Elizabeth would dress up, too, and Nicole would take the lead in creating wonderful dramatic play. Elizabeth never initiated such play, but was more than happy to go along with Nicole's theater. Great toys can buy great friends. And it only takes one or two good friends to make a significant difference in a child's life.

Questions from well-meaning friends and family like, "So, what does your child want for Christmas/his birthday, etc." can be quite a dilemma.

Want or need? For them or for attracting friends? Many mothers relate how many younger siblings eventually took the unwanted presents for themselves and that led to other problems. Autism affects everything, especially holidays.

Potty Training

Perhaps oughtism is most significant when it comes to toileting issues. So often we hurry the child because of our own timetable or our own sense of pressure. Tina, a friend of mine, was told by her behavioral specialist when her son was 4 that toileting issues are one of the most important things that you need to focus on, because it is one of the first things that children will notice about each other in terms of differences. A child who is potty trained immediately looks down on other children who have not yet achieved this milestone. Potty training for children with high-functioning autism seems to fall into two groups of children: those who are potty trained early and those who are very late.

We were in both groups because of Elizabeth and Ray's sensitivities. At 18 months, Elizabeth had had a bad diaper rash, so we were letting her play outside on the back lanai, or covered porch, stark naked. She peed, and I will never forget the look of absolute horror on her face as the urine ran down her leg. I cleaned her up and took her to the bathroom, where I showed her the insert toilet seat we had been given. I had read the manuals that suggested that the toilet seat be presented to the child, but not pressured. She immediately sat on it and released some more urine. She and the potty were bonded. I hadn't planned it, but I was pleased.

I had picked an insert toilet seat that fit into the "big potty" for several reasons. I knew that she did not handle transitions well, and it would be a fight to get her used to the baby potty seat only to move her over to the big potty. Also, we traveled quite a bit and I didn't want to be lugging the baby potty seat around. And finally, having a baby potty seat would involve me handling feces, and I was completely grossed out by that idea.

Poop just brings out my own sensitivities and makes me squirm. I was all for the portable insert.

However, there were unexpected problems. The first time Elizabeth pooped in the potty, the water splashed up and hit her on the bum. She screamed, cried, and consequently refused to poop in the potty for the next 2 ½ years. She was 4 years old before she would poop in the potty. She would go get a diaper, poop, and then insist on having her diaper changed. When I refused after a while, she would put the diaper on by herself, and then change herself into big girl panties. I once took the diapers away from her and refused to help her. I was fed up and told her that she had to use the big girl potty and that diapers were not an option. She continued to do the "I gotta go" dance and I ignored her pleas. I then saw her disappear, and reappear, looking happier, and then I realized that she had not actually gone in the direction of the bathroom. Yup, she had pooped behind the couch. I lost my cool, my husband, James, helped me realign myself, and we backed off. She did eventually potty when we moved houses, and she took to the bathroom as though there had never been a problem. However, to this day, she misses diapers and looks longingly at them.

Ray was almost completely opposite. Being male, he didn't get urine all over himself when he was naked. He did hate the feeling of poop on himself, though, and he did not get splashed when he first tried the potty around 2 years old. I soon learned to recognize "the look" when he needed to poop, and we would race off to the potty and reward him for doing so. He soon happily pooped in the potty. However, he was completely unaware of peeing and never let us know. I tried rewards, regular visits to the bathroom, floating targets, big boy underwear, reading books . . . nothing seemed to help. My children had the same teacher at the Montessori school they attended, and she and I laughed that between the two of them, there was a completely potty-trained child. One would pee and the other poop, but getting it together in the same child was a trick.

Ray was finally potty-trained one day when I resorted to character Pull-Ups because of an upcoming trip. The Pull-Ups alternated Spiderman, his favorite, and the Incredible Hulk. The first day, I realized that we had made a terrible mistake because he was *thrilled* to pee in the Spiderman Pull-Ups; he was excited to have them and asked to have them. The next day, I pulled out the Hulk Pull-Ups and he pulled away in fear. "*No*, Mommy! *No!*" I quickly threw the package behind me that had the next Spiderman Pull-Up and told him that the Hulk was the only kind of diaper we had, and he was going to have to pee in the Hulk ones. "*No*, Mommy! *No!*" He was really crying now in terror and fear. I was so sympathetic and even loved on him, but kept insisting that the Hulk Pull-Ups were the only ones we had left. If he wanted diapers, he would have to use them. However, if he wanted to pee in the potty, he could wear his Spiderman "big boy" underwear. I'll never forget his little teary voice as he said, "I pee in the potty, Mommy. I pee in the potty." And literally, from that moment on, Ray never had an accident. We laughed that we potty trained him through fear and intimidation, but it wasn't fear of us, it was the fear of Hulk. Sometimes you use what you have to in order to get them past a developmental milestone.

Other children with autism have had much greater issues with toileting. Because some children with autism have problems identifying cues from their own body, they may not recognize when they have to go to the bathroom. Similarly, teaching them to feel "proud of themselves" may be something they are not capable of understanding. Finally, they are so resistant to change in their routines that moving from a diaper to the bathroom is a major hurdle for them. Some suggestions include:

- Know that it will take a long time. Most toileting manuals suggest a period of a few weeks to a few months. Be patient and know that it *will* happen—just slower, and with greater consistency.
- Introduce the bathroom and potty in stages. Let him learn the word for bathroom; reward him for coming in the bathroom; sit on the potty dressed for a while, then present how to take down clothes in stages. It helps during this time to have clothes that are easy to get in and out of.

- Go to the bathroom often. Some programs recommend every 15 minutes, and one program I read about had the instructor play with the child in the bathroom during the regular times when bowel movements were more likely to occur. There is a potty-shaped watch available from One Step Ahead that little children can wear that beeps as often as you want it to—every 15 minutes for example—and reminds children to go.

- Make going to the bathroom a visual reminder. The key is to be firm and consistent—make going to the bathroom a part of the daily routine and remind the child visually with a cue. Friends of mine do the sign language "T" for "Toilet" to remind their son. That way, it's a reminder without drawing attention to him.

- Reduce distractions so that they can focus on what they have to do. For years, my son thought that his belly button was the "on" switch for peeing. I think that he was aware of muscle sensation in his groin and assumed that he could make it happen by massaging his belly button and focusing on that sensation.

Missing the Old Map

"Oughtism" rears its ugly head at most major transitions, developmental points, and sometimes completely out of the blue. I remember going home and crying when I was at a park one day with my children when they were 2 and 3, looking for manatees in the canals. I was excited, and they were much less so—more interested in the swings than peering into the murky waters below the bridge. A younger child, who I found out was 20 months old, toddled over to me and asked, "What are you doing?" I explained that I was looking for manatees, and he proceeded to tell me about his fish and the moon he had seen last night and how the moon wasn't really made of cheese, and on and on. When his mother rushed over full of apologies for his "bothering me," I told her that her baby was quite advanced in language. I turned away from my own silent daughter with tears in my eyes, knowing that I would never apologize for her chattiness.

Oughtism is part of the grieving process, and it is important to recognize that we grieve at different points in different ways for incredibly long times. Elizabeth Kubler-Ross (1969) noted that grieving follows a cycle and professionals often note that parents of children with special needs follow the same cycle. However, not everyone follows the same order or the same length of time. It can become important for spouses to understand that the other one may be in quite a different stage of grieving and that it is important to remain connected and communicative. Also, if any of these stages become too intense, please seek therapy. Therapists are trained to help people move to healthy ways of dealing with grief. Their expertise and, sometimes, medication may be necessary for you to be able to help your child.

First, there is anger where you might be angry at God, the professionals for not helping early enough, or the "mistakes" that you made. Anger provides initiative, but it often quickly moves to denial.

Denial is part of the process as parents wonder if everyone was wrong and this child really is fine. Often, after diagnosis, parents will be frozen in denial, not certain how to go about getting started, and not wanting to get started. It can happen when a parent just can't follow through on professional recommendations or not read the materials that are given to her.

I felt the pulls of oughtism and depression deeply during this phase. Denial also happens when parents jump on a bandwagon of a strategy that "everyone" is trying. They tend to look for immediate consequences and actions, rather than really focusing on the needs of their individual child. The new therapy has the promise of taking away the autism altogether, so parents join up, thinking that this will fix it and that all will be well soon. Finally, denial can lead to parents not being able to process all of the information that they need to. They can hear only portions of the information and ignore or discard the rest. It is important if you know that you are in this stage, or it feels too overwhelming, to remind the professionals that you will need to hear this again.

Bargaining often is the next stage. It is when parents start gathering as much information as possible on the issues surrounding autism. There is the feeling that if we just learn enough, we can beat this thing. If we do the right thing, we will come through this. And so parents bargain and search and become completely absorbed by this issue that they are determined will not get the best of them. It is during this time that parents can ignore their own needs and other needs of their family as well. Also, because they are learning so many different things, they may bombard their child with a variety of different therapies, minimizing the effectiveness of any one of them.

Accompanying each of these stages is depression. What ifs and maybes attack at night and interrupt your sleep. Second thoughts, blame, and tiredness all mix together to create a person that you and your spouse may not recognize any more.

The final stage is acceptance and it occurs when you realize that there is a "new normal" in your life: that things have gotten better and that you have accommodated. The acceptance stage doesn't last forever, and the full cycle of grief can be triggered again by a birthday, your friend's child getting a driver's license, a wedding you attend—any event in which you see the differences between your life and your "dream life" that you wanted—the reason you got married, had children, or went to college.

All of us have dreams of when we "grow up" and having a child with a disability rarely figures into that dream. But the periods of normality *will* get longer and the periods of grieving will get shorter and less intense.

FINDING A NEW NORMAL

We often are given the belief in our world that "If you do the right things, things are going to be GREAT!" In my educational, generational, and socioeconomic levels, we are led to believe that we can have it all: the great career, the great house, the perfect child. We read and read that if we avoid drugs at childbirth, eat organic, watch educational shows, breastfeed, wear seatbelts, and put our children on their backs, that we will be OK—we can avoid so many of the mistakes that our mothers made. Somehow disability has been perpetuated as a "mistake" and if you do everything right, then you should be protected. When misfortune does strike, there is a tendency to whisper and to look away. In fact, a 2009 study by Dr. Yamamoto and colleagues from the Harvard-affiliated McLean Hospital found that women in particular do not like to look at babies with deformities—they glance away and reject the pictures. We feel pain and discomfort for things that disturb our image of perfection.

As human beings, we are born with an innate sense of normal, and our children are especially dependent on the illusion of stability. Any change to that normal and our children react. What I have learned is that the times during change are incredibly hard. We hold on until we can sense a "new normal" coming. James and I will sometimes ask each other, "So, is that new normal here yet?" We have tried not to grieve the old normal, but to hold on—normal's coming. It's a wonderful way to sustaining each other and our family as we strive toward a routine. But normal takes time and sometimes it takes help. There are variety of ways to achieve it and lots of information to take in.

Down the Rabbit Hole 4

STUCK IN THE TRAP OF AGE-APPROPRIATE VS. ABILITY-APPROPRIATE

Let me just start by telling you that Elizabeth is "cured" of autism. I use "cured" in quotes, not because she got over a dread disease, but because she no longer qualifies for services because her speech is age-appropriate, her practical living skills are strong, and her social skills are only slightly delayed—and her academic abilities are far above grade level. She falls into that group of children whose mothers, doctors, and others claim are "cured" of or "recovered from" autism. Of course, she received a tremendous amount of therapy, we provide an intensive amount of coaching in a structured home environment, and she works *very* hard to master tasks that are set before her. Is autism gone? No, but we can live with it now.

There are many, many strategies and therapies currently available out there—most cost money and only a few are well-researched. A Google search of "autism treatments" found more than 315,000 pages devoted to this topic alone, whereas "autism cures" had almost 2 million sites. Clearly, there is no one right answer. And the debate between "treatment" and "cure" is a hotly debated one as well. A 2009 study by Dr. Deborah Fein and colleagues found that up to 20% of children with high-functioning autism who receive intense interventions are "recovered" by age 9. Being one of those statistics, I certainly advocate intensive treatment. Some people have told us that Elizabeth never "really" had autism; she just grew out of odd behaviors. Others have stated that she had "temporary autism." A well-known blogger, Dr. Polly Palumbo (2009), stated that she worries that the recovery of children who were diagnosed with high-functioning autism might give false hope to parents with more severe, intractable autism.

I don't really care if she grew out of it, or if she was cured—I only know that she got better, and I truly believe that we headed off significant issues by doing lots of things. And I also know that we're still dealing with issues—just not severely enough for continued professional treatment.

When Elizabeth was 4, we moved and changed states. In the new state, the IEP team determined that she didn't need occupational therapy. After about 6 months, the speech therapist told us that because she was then "within age-appropriate limits of speech," she no longer qualified for services for autism. That meant that my daughter had "beaten" autism after 2 ½ years of intense therapies. I didn't know whether to cheer or cry. I was thrilled that Elizabeth had made progress. But I knew that there was still so much more to go.

I asked her if she felt that Elizabeth was speaking at her *ability* level and was told, "No. She's very bright. But since she's speaking at the level of a 4-year-old, she doesn't need services any more." I was, and still am, so angry at a system that would give up on a child simply because she met a certain low level. Never mind that she was able to problem solve and analyze and could read already, but did not have the language level equivalent to all of that. Never mind the fact that social skills were still a foreign language to her. I was now on my own with her interventions.

Since then, I have had her tested so that I could have numbers to back up my intuition. Schools often just pat parents on the head when a parent says, "My child is very bright but has some challenges." Her IQ test, which overall was not high enough to qualify her for a gifted program, showed her visual processing abilities to be in the 99th percentile—higher than 99% of other children her age! Her language processing speed? Twenty-fifth percentile—below 75% of other children her age. And her achievement levels? All above grade level. She did not qualify for gifted services, although the psychologist told us that she "was gifted—clearly." She did not qualify for special education. We are on our own at this point. Does she still have autism? Officially no. Is autism impacting her growth and development? Oh yes . . .

The place where a child is now will be different tomorrow, the next day, and next year. People ask me sometimes how I see autism affecting her as she grows up, and I'm reluctant to answer. Autism was the last thing I expected and learning to deal with it has continually surprised me. Every time I feel myself relaxing into a pattern, something comes along to remind me that we are not a typical family. We went out to eat just last week, and ended up with Ray having a meltdown, hysterical tantrum because the chicken wasn't cut up right, which set off my daughter who cried because the noise was so loud. All families have sibling challenges and all families have restaurant challenges, and ours is no exception, but ours can be set off for different reasons. But then we went home and Elizabeth asked for a back rub—something unheard of 6 years ago. As I was rubbing her back, I said, "Boy, you hated this as a baby!" To which she replied, "Mama, I don't like it when other people touch me. But you're family."

I prepare for the worst and hope for the best. Autism will be something that my children deal with in so many aspect of their lives. Do I worry about them? Of course—that's my job. I'm a mom.

As a parent, I needed to know that there were lots of things that could help my child. The question is of course, what? What do I buy, use, try, believe? When I was searching the "University of Google," the problem wasn't finding information; the problem was too much information out there for me to process. I was already trying to process *why* this happened, my guilt over what I could have/should have/might have done, and *what* was going to happen, that I was completely overwhelmed by the amount of strategies for what I *could* do. The amount of information is staggering, and when researching I often shut down in frustration, feeling completely overwhelmed, only to log back on the next day. I can completely relate to Elizabeth's need to shut herself in her closet and rock herself until she feels less overwhelmed.

It is important to do your own research. But do talk with other parents! As Karyn Seroussi (2002) said:

> I . . . learned that an open-minded parent with an autistic child and Internet access could learn more about the biology of autism than a closed-minded clinician with twenty years of experience in developmental disabilities, and that other parents were a better resource for practical advice than professionals. (p. 124)

Keep a balance between science and story, parents and professionals, and go with your instinct as long as it doesn't hurt you, your family, or your child.

I'm not here to tell you what you can/could/should/might do. I encourage you to do what I do: research, do more research, talk to your family, and find a professional who listens to you and gives you advice that you can live with. Most importantly, find a professional who believes in the abilities of your child as much as you do or who is open to learning more. Children with high-functioning autism break a lot of stereotypes and professionals have to be willing to believe that some behaviors are not "problems" but are symptomatic of ability as well.

And know that you might have to change professionals. And change yet again when your family has learned all you can from that one. Every child on the spectrum is unique, and every family situation is unique. What works for one child may not work well for another. There is no one "best" strategy. Trust your instincts, trust your child, and trust that the professionals really are doing their best.

However, while professionals may know their strategy or the latest research in their particular area, and other parents may have had their own successes or insights, they do not know your child as well as you. You are the only one who sees your child in the holistic context and sees him or her progress from birth to adulthood. *No one* knows the track your child has followed, the progress she's made, or the implications on her whole life experience like you.

You are an expert on your child.

There is a wonderful phrase, "Go with your gut." Some fascinating research by the Harvard Medical School (2009) has suggested that the 30 feet of intestines in your body actually have their own system of nerves that are independent of the other nerves and that communicate directly with the brain. Called the enteric nervous system, it's a hotline connecting emotions, digestion, and brain functioning. You really do "know it in your gut" and experience "gut-wrenching" hurt, while poor decisions can "make you nauseous." Your gut may, indeed, know the right choice before your brain.

The goal is to find a match between your child and a strategy. And when your child changes, the strategy may have to change as well.

To further confound the issue, there is a deep divide between families who insist that they are "defeating" the enemy of autism as a disease and families who argue that their child is an enrichment or a blessing to them and that autism is a form of diversity. They argue that "neurotypicals" do not appreciate the strengths that autism can bring, while the other side seeks to alleviate the causes of autism. They are two different philosophies and both have very clear and vocal advocates.

As for me, I just wanted my daughter to get better and to love and appreciate her at the same time with all of her differences. The dual nature of autism is just like the dual nature of light—both a wave and a particle, both a disease and a way of being. But the road map you choose will depend on your understanding of autism, the research you undertake, what you feel you can do, and the professionals you work with.

Finding the Geographers

It is very important for you to find a professional who will listen to you—just as it is important for you to have a list of things to tell and ask the professionals. We interviewed several speech therapists who all immediately jumped into "textbook" mode and told me what I was supposed to be doing, without listening to me first. I got so tired of the "Oh, and you need to . . . " or "You might try . . ." statements from more polite therapists. We already *were* putting subtle pressure on our child to encourage talking. We already *were* being consistent with discipline and not giving into tantrums. We already *were* putting pictures around for her to point to in order to communicate. I was raised a good Southern girl who never talks back, and I'll never forget the speech therapist I finally told off when she said, "You need to be encouraging her to talk, but not pressuring her too much that it shuts her down." I finally snapped and said, "We *do*, damnit! I want to know what *else* I can be doing!" Zeppelin, the therapist we went with, was the first one who asked, "So, tell me what you've been doing with your daughter." Here was a partner in the process, not an "expert."

The other element I learned to look for was the therapist who truly wanted to learn about my child *before* she started working with her. I was so irritated the day a speech therapist said, "Wow . . . you know, she really responds when you tell her *why* you're doing something." I had previously told the therapist that Elizabeth really wanted to understand why she was supposed to be doing an activity, not just to do it. I knew that explanations helped her ability to stay engaged. I had told the therapist that as well. It was not the first time I felt shuffled aside as "Oh, that mom . . ."

Professionals often perceive parents as emotional and unable to separate their love for their child from their decision-making process. I was guilty enough as a teacher myself, listening to parents say that their child was completely misunderstood—that the problem wasn't their child, it was the teacher/school/system/other students . . . anything other than their own child or their own parenting. It wasn't until I became a parent myself of a child with a difference that I fully understood the pain of being told that there's something wrong with your baby and you might be the cause. Now, when I talk with parents, I don't use the disability label, or focus on what's "wrong" with their child. I talk about how the school/society/other children are very different than their child, and what's not working is the "fit" between all of these components.

It also is important to teach society, teachers, and other people about accepting people with autism. I recently heard a story of a mother, who when she explained that her son was yelling because he had autism, was told, "Well, he should wear a sign or something." Clearly, our society has a long way to go to understanding differences. But, we also can work on helping our beloved children fit in as well. And you play a key role in that process.

You have the right to be listened to as an equal partner in the process. You should feel comfortable sharing with and educating the professional about your child. You should feel confident that the professional really listened to you and made a fair decision based on her expertise and what you share. You should be able to trust that she is listening and not ridiculing. And you need to change professionals if you don't. Your responsibility is to be clear, and to be informative, to follow her suggestions for working with your child, and to listen—and to change professionals if it's not a good fit. *Your* responsibility is to do the best for your child you can.

For example, Elizabeth was being evaluated for her aptitude by the occupational therapist. She was in a hyperanxious state and I asked if I could be present. The therapist first gave Elizabeth four small colored blocks and then gave herself four blocks and she asked Elizabeth to make the same shape she did. She made an L shape with the blocks and said, "Now, you make that." Elizabeth just sat there, looking hard at the blocks and idly fingering them—appearing to be unresponsive. Knowing my daughter, I waited and finally said to the therapist, just as she was going to make a 0 on that question, "She's looking for the white one. You gave her different colored blocks than you have. She's trying to make the exact same as you and can't with different colors." "Oh!" said the therapist, and gave Elizabeth the same colors, who immediately made the same shape *and* color combination. Details are highly important to Elizabeth and she notices small things—someone with expertise in autism should have known that. It made me really wonder how many kids are misdiagnosed or underestimated simply because the therapist didn't know how a kid's mind worked. Or because the mom isn't pushy enough.

BY AIR AND BY SEA, ON FOOT AND ON WHEELS

No matter what vehicle you use for treatment, it is important to keep in mind that everyone has the same goal: helping your child improve. Now, some will aim for curing, others will aim for improvement; some are doing studies to make advances to the field, and others are trying to make money. There are passionate advocates for many of these various treatments who believe deeply in one approach, and there are others who are trying to debunk myths and use data in their decisions.

Intensive and Intentional Parenting

It cannot be overstated that the first line of therapy or help that you can do is what *you* provide. Parenting a child with high-functioning autism is intense—his responses are dramatic, his anger more intense and often, and you are left wondering if what you're doing is making any difference.

The answer is YES! YES! In fact, intensive parenting is the best form of therapy for these children and they, perhaps even more than typical children, *need* the parent to read to them, to share their quiet spaces, to connect with them, to help guide them through the tough times and to love them really, really hard, particularly when loving them is difficult. In other words, be a mom—really *be* a mom!

In his book *The Mind Tree*, Tito Mukhopadhyay (2000) discussed how much work his mother did—she read to him, she tried diets, she taught him to ride a bike, and she never gave up on him. In a battle about whether they were going to go to his uncle's wedding, Tito communicated with her that she had to choose between her brother and her son. "For you, I give my life. For him, I give three days," she responded (p. 64).

Perhaps the hardest part of parenting intensely is the lack of overt response that you may get from your child. You know that she loves you in the way that she may cling to you at times, but feeling intense love when there is no eye contact can be difficult. Talking to a child and engaging in communication with a child who doesn't talk back can be very difficult. Continuing on in the face of silence and pain can be overwhelming.

However, I cannot emphasize how key you are—you often provide the first translation to the rest of the world for your child. Tina, a friend of mine, shared how she would spend her afternoons at the grocery store, engaging in conversations with her son: pointing out colors of food, sounds of carts, and watching the toy train move around the top of the store. Her son would jump at the thunder sound that happened when the sprinklers watered the vegetables, and she would laugh, showing him that it was all right. She talked about rain, about textures, about shapes to him, helping him over and over to unite his perceptions with language. He is functioning so well now at the age of 13 that he no longer qualifies for autism services and some professionals she's working with question if he "really" had autism. She, and I, fully believe that "parent therapy" is the most effective form of intervention that you can provide.

Although I was blessed with a child who hugged and kissed, and looked me in the eye, I did face the inherent difficulty of teaching someone to talk and how to acclimate to her environment. We read, and we read, and we read. Elizabeth soon learned that I would stop anything I was doing if she appeared with a book in her hand. I would sit down on the nearest chair or even the floor, take her in my lap, and I would read it to her. Through reading, she listened to my voice and looked intensely at the pictures. There are many "baby" books I cannot now throw away because I have such sweet memories of reading them to my children, over and over again.

Similarly, once we realized that we were going to have to teach her how to talk, we started trying to work around the verbal part and focus on the communication aspect. I found pictures of common foods, laminated them, and taped them on the refrigerator so that Elizabeth could ask for what she wanted by pointing, rather than just screaming ineffectually. We asked her question after question and gave her choice after choice to give her opportunities to talk. "Do you want the cheese or the grapes? Do you want the pink dress or the blue one? Do you want to go fast or slow?" Each forced choice, question, and visual cue was an effort to reach her, to get her involved in our world.

And sometimes, I just stopped and enjoyed her and tried to see things the way she saw them. If her attention was caught by a passing train, I watched it, trying to see it through her eyes—the blur of the cars, the rhythmic clack of the rails—and I would find myself nodding and bobbing as well, in total sympathy with her feeling that this was a moment in which the world was ordered and safe and in rhythm. I let her swing and swing and swing, feeling the swaying of the world as it rushed past her, the brush of the wind, the head rush on the way back. I too felt the lure of thoughtlessness and only experienced sensation along with her. But I always knew that it was my job to bring her back to the world that, in the words of Tito Mukhopadhyay (2000), is "a suitable place for the social beings and not beings like us" (p. 124).

It also is the task of intensive parenting to track changes in your child. Tina still has her notebook of charts and graphs that she maintained on her refrigerator. For 3 years on a daily basis, she tracked bowel movements, behaviors, and medication intake. I kept lists of words spoken and activities to try at home. And I researched and I researched and I researched—thinking there was something else I could try to help me at home, and ultimately, to help Elizabeth.

The following is a list of treatments I either sought out or researched. I have divided these into the different means that are used: the different approaches therapies can take, the various specific therapies available, and the environments in which therapies can take place. Please do *not* use this as an exhaustive list! There is so much autism research out there that my list is going to be outdated within weeks. Also, many of the treatments are controversial to some degree. I'm a great believer in throwing the whole shebang at a problem. The hard part was deciding what to try and what to spend my time, money, and energy focusing on. My mother offered to do reiki—energy healing work that reeks of "woowoo" New Age stuff and that she seems to have a very strange knack for. Go right ahead! My husband's aunts went to Cyprus to get a silver icon that has been blessed by the Greek Orthodox Patriarch. Wonderful! My girlfriend included my daughter's name in her Prayer Circle. Fantastic! We opted for speech and occupational therapy as well as Montessori education. We did *not* do chelation or the GFCF (gluten free/casein free) diet. The stuff that did not take up my time or money, I was more than happy to accept. I learned early in my life never to laugh at other people's "magic" because sometimes magic does happen. And my daughter improved and that was magic to me.

PHILOSOPHICAL APPROACHES: INSTINCT, MIND, OR BODY

Applied Behavior Analysis

This is the gold standard of autism treatment. ABA is the system through which children are taught to stop doing inappropriate behaviors and to use appropriate behaviors using rewards. It is a very clearly established process by which a target behavior is determined, the steps to reach that behavior are identified, and the child is rewarded when he begins to come close to that desired behavior. It's a process of breaking down a goal into very specific steps to master first. It's very similar to the system your grandmother used when she said, "When you eat all of your dinner, you can have dessert." Structured by Dr. Ivar Lovaas in the 1960s (see Lovaas, 1987, for more information) for treatment of children with special needs, ABA principles have been found over and over again to work for kids with autism. It's the most successful treatment and is even recommended by the U.S. Surgeon General (n.d.). It's often the *only* thing to help students with low-functioning autism. The philosophy has many names—discrete trial teaching, behavior modification, stimulus-response—but any program that uses the words "behavior" or "skills" in it is probably rooted in this philosophy.

ABA believes that kids will respond to reinforcers that they want. Schools typically will use ABA in their approach to teaching. They will offer rewards and consequences to encourage children to behave, learn, and engage socially. I have seen a kid stop making moaning sounds for 5 minutes in order to get a Skittle. I have seen kids learn to point in order to get the lollipop afterward. ABA does not care *why* kids change their behavior; just that they do. There also are some amazing computer programs that have emerged out of this philosophy (collecting points and getting scores are used in these programs as forms of reinforcers). These cutting-edge computer programs teach kids with autism what to say in different social situations, to identify people's emotions on their faces, and to replace repetitive motions, such as hand flapping, with more socially acceptable ones, such as foot tapping.

There are many people who object to ABA for several reasons, one of which is that it is very similar to animal training. Whether you're teaching a child to say "Hello" at appropriate times and rewarding him with hugs and praise or teaching a dog to "come" with treats, ABA uses the same foundational principles of rewarding appropriate behaviors and then fading the reward once the behavior has been learned. I used to laugh that I got a puppy at the same time I started my teacher education program, and the dog's obedience classes and my discipline classes were very similar. I was a better teacher because I was a dog owner. In her 2006 book, *Animals in Translation*, Temple Grandin noted that she often feels more at home with animals than she does people—she understands how they react to things. Now, I happen to adore my dog and have no issues recognizing the underlying similar motivations in both of us. But others do.

The other concern that some people note is that ABA works on the symptoms, but not the underlying causes or issues. You can teach specific skills, but because generalization is so difficult for children on the spectrum, they often don't move those new skills forward on their own. I personally use ABA as a tool, but I much prefer cognitive interventions, because they allow the child to use her own cognition to help herself.

Cognitive Intervention

On the other side of the spectrum and with a lot less research on children with autism, cognitive interventions focus on metacognition, or teaching children to plan and to think "outside" themselves about their own thinking. Such strategies have been found to be highly effective for children with emotional and learning disorders, and for children with obsessive-compulsive disorders (OCD), but there is less research in children with autism. In children with obsessive-compulsive disorders for example, Dr. John Marsh (2006) found that when children are taught to "talk back" to themselves (and when they could realize that their compulsions were simply the manifestations of OCD, *not* a measure of their own capability of as a person), they were able to reduce obsessive actions and thoughts more effectively than with medication: "I'm not really wanting to check the light switch/oven/wash my hands again. It's just the biology of the OCD that is making me think I need to. I can outwait the chemicals that are firing in my brain."

Similarly, when children with learning disabilities are taught how to plan to learn—"What do I need to do first? What should I do after that?"—rather than just doing something, they become better at managing their own learning. Studies by Karen Harris and Stephen Graham (1999), for example, have found that time after time, teaching children to plan out the process through which they're going to do something is incredibly effective at raising their performance. They have found that children with multiple types of language processing problems often have huge growths in thinking when they are taught specific steps and questions at each step. It's hard to do without training because it can devolve into the frustrated screech of a mother who asks, "WHY did you do that?!"

Cognitive intervention does, however, assume that children have a certain degree of theory of mind: they can plan ahead, separate themselves from their behavior, and recognize that other people behave and think differently than they do. Such abilities are not always present in children with autism. But can they be used and taught? I certainly believe so!

In our house, we use both strategies of ABA and cognitive intervention. Elizabeth and Ray are rewarded for completing their work, for doing dishes, or for sitting in their seats at restaurants. They get computer time taken away if they have a tantrum. But often, I ask them, "What can do you do?" "What might happen and what can you do about it?" "What do you need to plan for?" "If you feel a tantrum coming on, what can you do instead?" We have lists of steps visually represented for tasks like "clean your room," "feed the dog," and so on to help them visualize what tasks they are responsible for and increase their positive behaviors.

Elizabeth really responds to this kind of instruction. For example, when she was a baby, she *hated* the sand on her toes; she would try to climb up me if I bent to put her on the sand. It was such a drag to live near the beach and not be able to go. One day, I got a rock and brought it to her in the backyard. She looked it over and I pointed out things about it—it was bumpy and hard. We pulled on it a bit and little pieces of it came off.

In a very excited, happy voice, I told her, "Look Elizabeth! The rock crumbles! It gets smaller!"

Then, I brought out some sand in a bucket and she pulled away, not about to put her hand in it. "It's OK, darling. You don't have to touch it. But LOOK! Sand is little rocks. It's the rock all smooshed up into little pieces. Can you crumble the rock? You're making sand! What a great, strong girl you are!"

Very tentatively, Elizabeth reached back to the rock, put her hand on it, and looked carefully at the sand. I exclaimed in a really excited tone, "That's right! Sand is just little teeny rocks. Smooshed rocks!"

After the third day, she put her hand, oh so carefully, into the sand. I said, in a very happy voice, "Smooshing rocks! That's what you're doing! Smooshing rocks!"

The next time we went to the beach, I reminded her ahead of time. "We're going to see sand. Remember what sand is? . . . (long pause for gentle pressure for possible speech interaction—didn't happen) . . . It's rocks all broken up and smooshed into sand! You can touch it just like you did rocks—all it is rocks, and you LIKE rocks! I know it feels yucky, but you just have to remember it's just rocks."

The first day at the beach was . . . quieter. She wouldn't let me put her down, but she leaned waaaay over in my arms to watch the sand. It didn't do anything scary and within 2 more days, she was down on it. I started this intervention when she was about 10 months old and it took her until she was more than 2 years old to really lose her fear of sand, after many reminders that the sand was just rocks. Now she builds sand castles and you might never guess she once hated it. But she won't bury herself it in nor dig her toes in it at the edge of the surf. But that's OK—we all have a great time at the beach!

Biological Approaches

There is a growing body of evidence that autism is caused by a complex set of genetic and environmental interactions, resulting in a whole host of protein and intestinal issues that lead to psychological challenges. For many years, there has been a deep division between psychological issues, which autism is classified under, and physical issues, which includes the study of disease and bodily functions. However, as anyone who gets cranky when they're hungry or fights with their husband when they're tired knows, there is a significant relationship between the mind and the body. While ABA and cognitive interventions focus on the management of the symptoms of autism, biological interventions focus on the management of the cause of autism.

The physical source of autism is hotly debated. In their excellent books, Jenny McCarthy (2006) and Karyn Seroussi (2002) trace the combinations of yeast, enzymes, various proteins, and food allergies that can cause autism. Seroussi noted that the combinations can cause opioids in the blood that look similar to when individuals are "tripping" on LSD and psilocybin (magic mushrooms), all variations of fungi. The sensory and behavioral differences of autism can look quite a bit like persons who are on hallucinogenic drugs.

One of the challenges, as Seroussi (2002) noted, is that the first people who adopted this mind/body connection for autism were perceived as "crazies" and cranks who did not do "real" science. Medical innovations become standard only when they follow a set of prescribed processes, such as double-blind studies. If this process is not followed, or is generated from people who are not experts in the field (such as parents without credentials), a treatment is quickly relegated to myth and quackery. Dr. William Shaw, founder of the Great Plains Laboratory, who advocates the control of yeast and candida in the treatment of autism and is quoted in Karyn Seroussi's book said, "My [initial] opinion of the 'yeast people' was that they were the same folks who claim to have been abducted by aliens" (p. 167). The view taken by many followers of alternative treatments for autism is that unproven or unsubstantiated does not equal false.

As a layperson, I have to admit that I didn't know what to make of all of the fierce arguments over the physical issues. I didn't know enough to make an informed decision and the amount of work it would take to become up to speed on these issues appeared daunting. Karyn Seroussi (2002) and Susan Senator (2005) had husbands with technical backgrounds. I didn't have that, and I decided that I would "feel" my way through the issues. Certainly, there are powerful arguments for the presence of yeast and other biological factors. However, many other scientists and organizations that I also respect tend to debunk these ideas rather frequently. There is so much research going on that I was unwilling to take a stand either way. I went with what appeared to work for *my* child. I have respect for all parents trying their very best to help their child, and I resent close-mindedness of any type. There appears to be a combination of biological and environmental causes and responses that can be taken. Twenty, 10, 2 years from now, I hope that we have a much clearer picture and that this argument is considered anachronistic, similar to arguing about how to cure polio—an epidemic of another time that has since been conquered.

Combining all of these theories we know about in real life? It's called parenting.

THERAPIES: MAIN ROADS AND BYROADS

Everything But the Kitchen Sink

We were open to most things that we came upon. We tried some and didn't try others. We balanced family needs, time, money, and our goals. We listened to a variety of people and read and read and read. I was determined that we were not going to try one thing for a week or two, just to try something else new again. I was committed to letting the strategies we chose work. Did we pick the best strategies? I have no idea. But given our time pressure, our money situation, our level of knowledge, and our needs, we did the best we could. Resource information for many of the therapies listed below is provided at the end of this book.

Speech Therapy

This is the first place almost all autism interventions start. I had heard stories upon stories about how 3-year-olds pester you with questions, and I was so sad that we weren't going to have that experience. I asked the speech therapist why that was so important, and she told me that without questions children can't learn and make connections. They ask questions for two reasons: (1) to get an answer, but also (2) to figure out what they want to know. Three-year-olds do not plan ahead and so they do not plan their questions until they ask them. It is through the very asking that they are learning how to learn. The answers are not nearly as important as the process of asking. I knew that it was key to engage Elizabeth in conversation, so I turned to a running monologue. "Da?" she would ask, pointing to the sky. "Oh honey, those are clouds. The big puffy ones are cumulus clouds. Isn't that a great word—cuuumuuuulous? They build up to make rain. Rain comes from clouds and the grayer the cloud, the more rain. If it's flat on top, those are called thunderheads and that's when we hear the big booms, and . . . " I would exhaust my entire knowledge of clouds and rain and try to provide as much information and language support as I could. To her credit, she would listen patiently (at least I always thought she was listening) and then turn and point to something else. "Da?" And I was off and running talking about kinds of cars. I truly had no idea what she wanted to know, and I hoped that somewhere in the enormous verbiage that I was giving her, she would get what she needed.

I've worked in schools most of my professional life and only occasionally worked directly with speech therapists. Had I to do it over again, I might go into speech therapy. The therapists we worked with were truly outstanding. They would work one-on-one with Elizabeth, bring out toys and games, and engage her in back and forth conversation. They would exert gentle pressure on her to talk. "Do you want the blue bear or the green bear?" "Boo." "Good girl! Here's the BLLLLUE bear!" I learned that I had to tell them to explain to Elizabeth what they were wanting her to do and she would be much more cooperative. From the beginning of her life it seems, Elizabeth wanted to know "Why?" (Something she probably inherited from her inquisitive parents! "Why" can sometimes be interpreted as questioning authority, when in reality, we truly want to know the meaning behind the question. I totally understood where she was coming from.) When we would explain to Elizabeth that she was sorting bears by color because we wanted to see how well she knew her colors, she would happily commence to sorting. Otherwise, she just sat and looked at you when you said, "Can you sort these bears by color, Elizabeth?"

When she turned 3, speech therapy moved to her school. They were focusing more on her use of language at that point and working with the teacher on using active strategies to involve other students in her activities. I would get a daily notebook back and forth that gave details.

When we moved to Pennsylvania, speech therapy was covered by our insurance company. Glory, glory! I was irritated that the thousands of dollars that we had paid in one state was covered by another, but oh well! Now, insurance companies are being pressured to help families with autism, and it can't happen fast enough in my opinion. Without speech therapy, I shudder to think of where we might be.

Many children on the spectrum of high-functioning autism, such as those with Asperger's syndrome, do not receive speech therapy until they are in elementary school. The speech therapy focuses not on the production of words, but on the use of words. Many children with Asperger's syndrome have a monotone, pedantic manner of speaking. Speech therapy then moves into a communication aspect in which children are taught listening skills and how to respond to what others say. Communication becomes a very cognitive task in which children are taught to listen for key words to which they respond.

In children with high-functioning autism, communication is not the easy automatic skill that it is with typical children and adults. For this reason, speech therapists are central figures in any form of intervention. They can teach the child to use his intellectual and analytical skills to break down the steps of communication and great progress can be made.

Occupational Therapy

This is really where Elizabeth's therapy got strange. She needed occupational therapy to help her learn to deal with the sensory input that was causing her to get anxious or afraid. She sat in pools of plastic balls, spun in swings, rolled on big therapy balls, listened to modulated music on headphones, and had to be "brushed" with a hard plastic bristle brush. The therapist listened to my questions patiently and explained how all of these are various calming and alerting techniques that can "wake up" or "calm down" neurological impulses that are being misinterpreted by the body. I was fascinated, and more than a little skeptical. Swinging was something we did at the park; how could these people take money for this? However, I did notice an improvement within months. Elizabeth could go to the beach. She wasn't wandering around aimlessly as much. She could calm down when I asked her to.

Related to occupational therapy, sensory rooms attempt to either stimulate a depressed sensory system or calm down an overanxious one. The first time I went into one, I was convinced that the person who first came up with this idea had done serious LSD in his or her time. The sensory room at the Home of the Innocents in Louisville, KY, has water bubbling in large floor-to-ceiling tubes, lit from within with lights that change color. Music that is very instrumental and vaguely Eastern in its tonal quality is played. The floor has sections of different textures. Elizabeth loved her experiences in her therapist's sensory room. We didn't do it often, but she enjoyed the room and appeared to be calmer when we left. Did it make a tremendous change in her? No . . . but it was worth trying. For many children, taking them to a place where their senses become overloaded in rhythmic manners can be intensely calming.

Floortime

Developed by Dr. Stanley Greenspan (see Greenspan & Weider, 2003), Floortime is a time of active engagement with a child with autism. I first learned about Floortime from the book *The Boy Who Loved Windows* by Patricia Stacey (2003), who worked extensively with Dr. Greenspan. We did not have the treatment available to us, but I read up on it considerably, bought the book, talked about it with our nanny Irene, and down on the floor we went with Elizabeth.

Floortime involves watching the child play and then following her lead with anything that attracts her attention—creating moments of engagement, or "circles of communication" through novelty and positive reinforcement. The emphasis isn't on skills, but on social engagement, with the attempt to increase the number of times your child communicates. You are to playfully interrupt your child's stimming or withdrawal, and attract her back to the world through lively, novel, and happy communication. We exaggerated our actions and our happy, positive emotions when we were talking with her to attract her attention. It is a highly stimulating form of playing with your child, and it is exhausting.

Never the most gregarious of people, I would tire quickly after about half an hour of talking in a very excited manner and trying to play with Elizabeth's toys with her. Luckily, our nanny, Irene, all of 17 years old at the time, excelled at this form of therapy. She had an amazing knack for making Elizabeth laugh. I would watch her open her eyes wide at Elizabeth, roll on the floor in reaction to any reaction of Elizabeth's, talk with a wonderfully dramatic voice with her, and give lots and lots of hugs and "high fives" when Elizabeth would respond. Irene was a natural at creating therapy moments, and although she wasn't formally trained in anything, she could think of activities and ways to communicate and engage with Elizabeth that I could not. I am deeply grateful to Irene, and include her in our list of professionals that I give credit to for pulling Elizabeth out of autism.

Chiropractic Therapy

I was at a "mommies group" one morning when we were just starting the process of identification. Elizabeth wasn't talking and hadn't said a word. My anxiety levels were off the charts. One of the other mommies said that she had just taken her daughter, who was just identified with autism, to Dr. Suzanne, a chiropractor who specialized in sacro-occipital therapy, related to craniosacral therapy. The other little girl was running around with the other children, laughing and screaming as they jumped in the pool together. I was frustrated because our appointment wasn't for another 6 weeks with Early Intervention, so I got Dr. Suzanne's name and number. Her reputation was sealed with me when I talked to our doula, Michelle, who had become a very good friend at this point. Michelle went to Dr. Suzanne, and so off we went.

Dr. Suzanne manipulated Elizabeth's back and head and seemed just to apply pressure in strange spots. Elizabeth was very squirmy on the bench and then went still. On the way home, she spoke her first word beyond the names of our family—"Seepy"—and she went to sleep right there in the car, something she *never* did. I sat at a red light and cried that I had heard my daughter's voice for the first time. Before this, she had used a garbled "Diddle-la" which meant both "Cody-dog" and "home," and she used nonverbal gestures, but never had she spoken a word out of the blue like that.

We continued chiropractic therapy even when we moved. In one really stunning visit at Dr. Paul's office, Elizabeth got manipulated when she had had a particularly trying day. She was sing-songy, stimming, and didn't seem to hear us. Any attempts to touch her made her pull away and giggle uncontrollably. She went up on the table, he pressed on the top of her head and inside her mouth. Elizabeth squirmed away, shrieked loudly, and then collapsed. She slept all the way home and woke up clearheaded and coherent.

Coincidence? Possibly. Was she a completely changed child after that? Not completely, but enough that we all ended up going to Dr. Suzanne and consequent chiropractors. I would feel strange ticklish feelings when she was working on me, and I felt significantly better afterwards. I don't really care if hard science shows that this works or not. It did for our family.

Prayer/Reiki

I put these two together because they both involve working with higher powers. Elizabeth's name was written on a card and prayed over by my husband's aunts. They lit candles and sent us icons blessed by the metropolitan, similar to an archbishop. My best friends included her name on their various prayer groups. And my mother did reiki.

Reiki is an Eastern healing energy that focuses positive growth on a particular illness or hurt. Mother, who is a scientist by training and holds a degree in geology, is a certified Reiki Master and has a very odd ability to diagnose and heal, called "intuitive healing." She sensed a "dark spot" in Elizabeth's brain near the Broca's area, related to language. She worked on lighting up those synapses, getting them to respond and connect. The momentous day that Elizabeth called me "Mommy" for the first time, my mother called me to see if there had been a change, even before I could call her to celebrate.

Again, coincidence? Possibly. Didn't matter to me at all. If higher powers, head adjustments, speech therapy, Floortime, and occupational therapies were working, we would stay with them.

As a professor, I would recommend to parents to try the strategies with significant documentation and evidence of effectiveness, such as ABA and speech therapy. As a parent, as long as you have the time, the energy, and the money, you should try what works best for your family and the techniques in which you see resulting improvement. But you absolutely should include strategies that are well-established and productive. Form a foundation of the well-established strategies and with the leftover time, energy, and money you have, try others as well.

OTHER KITCHENS, OTHER SINKS

There are a whole host of other things that we did not try. We did not try them because I didn't know about them then, the negatives of trying them outweighed the positives, or I was too busy trying other things that I simply didn't have time. I list them only to let people know that they need to do their own research to see if these strategies are things to try, believe, or reject. Parents need to be informed because professionals have such contradictory information. I am firmly of the belief that science can tell us a tremendous amount of information, but to quote Shakespeare, "There are more things in heaven and earth, Horatio/Than are dreamt of in your philosophy." What is now science was once magic, and what was once fringe is now mainstream.

Augmentative and Assisted Communication (AAC)

The range of technological innovations available today to children who are unable to talk fluently is boggling. From simulated voice technology to iPhone apps, such as Proloquo2go, that allow children to click on icons to make sentences, technology is making leaps and bounds to bridging communication barriers.

Text-to-speech technology allows the computer to do the talking for the child. When the child types, the computer then reads the material aloud to someone else. There is a wonderful YouTube clip by a woman named Amanda, who has severe autism, is completely nonverbal in oral speech (but maintains a blog called Ballastexistenz), and is institutional-ized, in which she stims, makes no eye contact, and provides a running computerized monologue. She shared how autism is "her language" then noted that she is treated differently because she does not communicate well in our language, yet no one tries to learn her language. Her thoughts are coherent, very logical, and fascinating to listen to. The computer is doing the "talking" for her, and you truly feel as though it is translating for you. Without the use of her computer and its voice, Amanda would appear to be noncommunicative and without thought at all. The computer provides a fascinating insight into the world of a person with autism.

However, technology is not the only means of allowing children with difficulty conversing to communicate. AAC can include visual schedules, the Picture Exchange Communication System (PECS), and Requesting Puzzles. All of these strategies tend to use a visual picture that the child selects to represent a word. The child can communicate with others using pictures rather than words. The key element of AAC is that the child *initiates* communication, and does not just respond to directions or situations; the beginning of the communication cycle is maintained by the child.

Son-Rise Program

A positively focused intensive therapy, the Son-Rise Program, offered through Autism Treatment Center training programs conducted through video workshops provided around the world, is based on the premise that autism is at heart a relational issue. As a result, it focuses on active, dynamic play therapy over the course of several 5-day workshops. Rather than stamping out stimming and repetitive behaviors, the parent or therapist joins the child in his activities, sharing the experience with him. Through a focus on increasing the motivation of a child, skills such as eye contact, vocabulary, and interactive attention span are developed and nurtured.

Biological Approaches

Biofeedback

Sometimes referred to as EEG biofeedback, neurotherapy, or brain wave therapy, biofeedback is a noninvasive computerized process that works to retrain brainwaves to function in a normal state, providing long-term results with minimal side effects. During biofeedback therapy, children wear electrodes on their head and learn to control video games by exercising the parts of the brain related to emotional regulation and attention. Considered alternative therapy, biofeedback seems to hold some significant promise as children literally learn to control their own brain functions. It is the biological feedback to teaching a child to pay attention to his own thinking processes. It is expensive and not covered under most medical plans.

Gluten Free/Casein Free (GFCF) Diet

This strategy is one that is getting a lot of attention lately. In her 2006 book, Jenny McCarthy stated that diet is what ultimately saved her son. Interestingly enough, there is quite a bit of information that supports the idea of diet as an intervention. Many children with autism also experience stomach, intestinal, or digestive issues—gas, constipation, and/or diarrhea. In other words, their tummies hurt. And more insidiously, they are not getting the nutrition they need or having adverse protein relationships in their systems that affect mental functioning. Dr. Stephen Porges (2007), in his polyvagal theory, has found a link between the nervous system, health of the digestive tract, and ability for social engagement and anxiety levels: Not only are you what you eat, but your friends are based on what you eat as well!

In the Gluten Free/Casein Free (GFCF) diet, gluten that is found in wheat and most binding agents, and casein, which is found in dairy products, are taken out of the diet. A sugar-free diet is just that—a removal of sugars and other carbohydrates—while yeast treatments remove unhealthy bacteria buildup and candida. Other diets restrict oranges, apples, tomatoes, red grapes, and bananas because of their high levels of phenols and sugars.

The yeast treatment often means the taking of Nystatin, a medication that does not go into the bloodstream but removes the yeast in a person's digestive tract. According to Jenny McCarthy (2006) and Karyn Seroussi

(2002), there are reports of "yeast die-off" in which the child has terrible diarrhea and behavior problems for a certain amount of time when they start the antifungal medication. There are some parents who report that once the yeast was out of their child's system, he showed remarkable improvement and a reduction in the "drunken walk" or the tippy toes gait that many children with autism exhibit.

Interestingly, according to many experts in allergy treatment, such as Dr. Ellen Cutler (2003), author of *The Food Allergy Cure*, one of the hallmarks of a food allergy is the craving for the very food that creates the problem. Many parents of children on the spectrum note that their child craves milk or pasta—dairy and gluten—and have a very restricted self-selected diet. Rarely do children on the spectrum crave popcorn or chocolate. Parents' arguments for cutting out casein and gluten often are that the child didn't have a balanced diet beforehand and that excluding those foods would allow the child to digest necessary vitamins and minerals better, without the "leaky gut" that the food allergies can create.

According to the organization Talk About Curing Autism (TACA, 2009), the results of the diets, according to many parents, is startling in how well and how quickly improvement is noted. Some parents notice improvement within days. Some see only small gains. Some see none. It is an investment in money, time, and creative cooking that can have tremendous payoff, but not always.

There is a great deal of debate about this type of intervention. The GFCF diet is listed under Autism Quackery on the Autism Watch site (http://www.autism-watch.org), and there is a deep divide between the Defeat Autism Now! (DAN!) group that advocates alternative treatments and the traditional medical community, both of which argue that the other side refuses to listen. The use of diet has even been used as "abuse" evidence in divorce cases. It certainly is confusing—following a sugar-free, gluten-free, casein-free, and phenol-free diet would leave a child with very little food options to eat. Parents have to research what works for their individual child if they decide to go down this route.

Supplements

Some advocates of autism propose that children be given large doses of magnesium and vitamin B6. Magnesium is needed for the proper functioning of every cell, particularly muscle and brain cells, while B6 is needed for more than 60 biological processes. Magnesium is found especially in green vegetables, seeds, nuts, and whole grains. Vitamin B6 can be found in avocados, liver, nuts, chicken, fish, wheat germ, and bananas. However (the theory goes), because children with autism are lacking digestive enzymes that help them process wheat, milk, and other foods, they do not get the proper amount of magnesium and B6 through diet alone.

Some parents provide magnesium supplements to their children through Epsom salt baths, in which magnesium is absorbed through the skin. The theory is that the enzyme that is needed to break down B6 is lacking in children with autism and that supplementation is needed to provide enough material for cell health.

Effectiveness data is mixed. Two small but well-controlled studies by Dr. Tolbert and colleagues (1993) and Dr. Findling and colleagues (1997) showed no effects, positive or negative, of vitamin B6 or magnesium therapy individually. One slightly larger, but less well-controlled preliminary study by Dr. Findling, cited in his 1997 study, showed positive and significant behavioral effects of combined vitamin B6 and magnesium. A very small, double blind study by Dr. Lelord and colleagues (1981) also found slightly positive effects of supplementing magnesium and B6. Magnesium is toxic at high levels, and too much B6 can cause nerve damage in adults, so care should be taken for proper dosing. I would highly recommend that you consult with your child's pediatrician before undertaking this therapy.

Chelation

Chelation is a treatment for acute heavy metal poisoning, such as mercury, iron-arsenic, lead, uranium, and plutonium. The chelating agent can be administered through an intravenous drip, a shot in the muscle, or a transdermal patch, or given in an oral medication. It typically is used in the case of industrial accidents or in warfare, when people have knowingly been exposed to heavy metal poisoning. Parents who believe that mercury in immunizations are the cause of their child's autism are the ones most likely to seek this out. However, chelation is considered to be quite dangerous, and has been largely abandoned since 2005 when Abubakar Tariq Nadama, a 5-year-old boy with autism, died during chelation because of a resultant elevated heart rate. This is the only therapy I would strongly discourage.

However, there are a number of websites that describe "natural chelators," such as cilantro, garlic, and methylsulfonylmethane (MSM; also known as dimethyl sulfone), a naturally occurring sulfur compound found in fresh vegetables, seafood, and meat. Suggestions for starting this therapy include "juicing" and eating lots of protein in order to flush out the heavy radicals in the body.

Hyperbaric Oxygen Treatment (HBOT)

Oxygen chambers have long been used for people who are recovering from "the bends" or an excess build up of carbon dioxide in their bodies, typically scuba divers who come up too fast. People breathe in extra oxygen in a pressurized chamber. According to Jordan Lite (2009), a writer for *Scientific American* citing a study in *BMC Pediatrics*,

> The randomized, double-blind controlled study of 62 children found that those who received 40 hours of treatment over a month were less irritable, more responsive when people spoke to them, made more eye contact and were more sociable than kids who didn't receive it. They were also less sensitive to noise (some autistic children experience a kind of sensory overload from loud sounds and background noise). The most improvement was observed in kids older than five (the study included children ages two to seven) who had milder autism. (p. 2)

However, the researcher, Dr. Daniel Rossignol, and his colleagues (2009) noted that there are some risks involved, including ear pain, reversible myopia (nearsightedness), and seizures. If parents do decide to consider HBOT before more research is completed, however, it makes sense to do so in the context of a formal autism clinic or children's hospital—both to ensure proper methodology and to reduce the risk of side effects. It is expensive and rarely covered under health insurance.

Magnet Therapy

Children who receive magnet therapy sit in a chair while a magnetic coil is placed near the scalp. This process creates an electric current that researchers say enhances the ability of specific cells to protect the brain from sensory overload in one region. Researchers at the University of Louisville Medical School (2009) have mapped how tiny strands of brain tissue, called cortical cell minicolumns, develop and connect. That research suggested defects in the minicolumns that interfere with information processing, and has created interest in the possible improvement with children with autism. Very new, the therapy only seems to result in mild headaches for the participants.

Medication

A whole range of medications are used to treat the symptoms of autism. There is no medication specifically for autism, but medications for depression, seizures, sleeplessness, anxiety, hyperactivity, and irritability all can help to control the problems associated with it. I would recommend that you work closely with a psychopharmacologist who can advise you about various side effects, dosages, and other issues you may face. It is critical that you keep track of the dosages and the effects on your child. A friend of mine, Tina, kept a behavior chart that noted timing and size of dose as well as timing of behavioral issues. She knew exactly when a medication kicked in, and when a medication did not appear effective. During any time when you are trying a new medication, be sure not to introduce any other new things into your child's system. Introduce new medications when you can follow your usual routine so that you can determine if any changes are indeed due to the medication and not the changes in your child's life.

Withholding Immunizations

This strategy isn't as much of a way of "treating" autism as it is "preventing" it. However, and this is the only area that I take a hard line stance on, it is extremely dangerous. As my grandmother, who has talked me through this whole process, said, "People just don't remember the iron lungs for polio."

That being said, I'm completely in favor of cleaning up the immunizations, moving to a different schedule, separating out the mega-immunizations that are given, or delaying giving a number of them. Jenny McCarthy (2006) has called for the Centers for Disease Control and Prevention to "get the crap out" of immunizations, and I couldn't agree with her more. The human body is so complicated and so powerful that it's ludicrous to imagine purposefully putting huge doses of dangerous ingredients into our babies. Clearly, there is a need to study the effect of large, massive infusions of drugs upon a developing, at-risk immune system. And what *does* an at-risk immune system look like and can we identify those children? The emphasis *needs* to be on identifying those children who are at risk for immunization overload, rather than blanket statements that a certain schedule of immunizations is right for everyone.

As a teacher, I quickly learned that there is no one instructional method that works for every child. Children develop in far too different ways, and there is diversity in human development of *all* kind. Certainly the same holds true for physical development as well—not every baby's system will be able to tolerate the immunization schedule. Should we continue to work to wipe out polio, measles, mumps, rubella, diphtheria, and chicken pox? Of course! Too many people have died from these diseases in the past. But does everyone need the same lock-step schedule of immunizations? Perhaps not everyone can tolerate the tidal wave of immunological response that combined immunizations provided in a short amount of time creates. Rather than engaging in the "Should we require vaccinations?" fight, shouldn't we be asking, "What children are at risk for vaccinations the way we're giving them?" Clearly, there is more research to be done!

But large chunks of my family died 80 years ago from flu that is treatable today. Rubella can cause a laundry list of disabilities in the unborn children of our children. Measles and mumps can cause terrible things in people who get them, including blindness, sterility, and death. A recent study in the journal *Pediatrics* by Jason Glanz and colleagues (2009) of the Institute for Health Research, found that one in 20 children who did get not get immunized came down with whooping cough, compared to 1 in 500 children who were immunized. And while no parents would want their child to get these terrible diseases, people feel safe not immunizing their children simply because so many people *do* immunize. However, counting on me to keep your child healthy places an unfair burden on me.

This is an issue on which so many people have staked out their viewpoints and what truly is needed is dialogue. As Karyn Seroussi (2002) said, "Arrogance is the recipe for error" (p. 145).

Let's just keep everyone as healthy as possible, shall we?

Everyday Strategies

Because children with high-functioning autism have intact cognitive abilities, there are a variety of everyday, household strategies that show promise of effectiveness because of their ability to use a child's mind effectively. As a family, we have learned a whole host of ways to cope and ease some of the challenges faced by autism. None of them work all of the time, but I try to think of them as a toolbox with different strategies I can use at different times.

Scripts

One of the first things I realized when Elizabeth started being able to talk was that while she could *make* the word, she couldn't always *find* the words. She didn't know what to say in certain situations. So, we practiced scripts.

Me: Elizabeth, when the lady at the store says "hello," you should say "hello" back to her.

Elizabeth: (nod)

Me: Let's practice. "Hello there, little girl!"

Elizabeth: Hello. (whispered)

Me: GOOD! Now, when the man at the restaurant says "Hello, big girl," what do you say?

Elizabeth: Hello?

Me: YES—same answer! Good! Now, and this one is trickier, but I know that you can do it. The lady says, "Hello little girl. How are you?" You don't say "Hello," you say "Fine." Listen for her voice to go up at the end. That means that she's asking a question and wants an answer. Let's practice, "Hello pretty thing! How are you today?"

Elizabeth: Fine?

Me: EXCELLENT!

We practice scripts for introductions, making friends, presentations in school, restaurants, ordering pizza . . . Every chance I get, I'm asking Elizabeth to speak, but making sure that we practice ahead of time. She's become quite good at combining scripts and most of her conversation looks typical. She has shown amazing determination and creativity at how she analyzes how scripts go together. My husband has even taught her conversational scripts in Greek so that she can converse with her aunts in Greece! Those scripts are much shorter, but I understand that she has an excellent accent—amazing for a kiddo who couldn't talk for so long!

Circular Conversations

One of the interesting strategies that my family has adopted because of our shared emotional sensitivities is a communication style we call "circular talk." When a subject that is going to cause tension, anger, or distress is necessary to talk about it, we allude to it—set the stage first. Then, we talk about something else. Then, we discuss it in general and then go off on yet another subject, or perhaps back to the first distracter. It pays to keep up with current events in my family—we use them as conversational fillers. Then, we work on more of the "real" conversation, only to dance away when emotion threatens. We chatter on about something else, give the other person time to recover and then go back to the topic, but in a problem-solving frame of mind. It's a well-timed dance of conversational skill that requires that you pay attention to when the other person can handle talking about the topic again. No screaming for us. No yelling, no overt shows of emotion. So many people in my family are fragile emotionally and feel things intensely, including Elizabeth. When Elizabeth feels anger, she is *angry*. When she's sad, she is intensely distraught. Autism? A member of our family? Perhaps our family has undiagnosed autism running through it? Southern heritage? Who knows? But circular conversations are our coping strategy and have been very effective with Elizabeth.

Crisis Books

I learned of this strategy from Susan Senator's (2005) book, although we have done this only a few times. However, I know of other parents who have used this strategy extensively. If you know of a situation that is coming up that is going to stress your child out—going to the doctor, Christmas, visiting Disney theme parks, anything that can be a novel and potentially frightening situation to your child—you can prepare him by creating personal books that he can look at about the new experience. The books can use pictures of the family or the child and should tell the child what is going to happen. We used this once for a move. Each sentence had a picture and the words were very simple.

> All of our stuff is going into boxes.
> Nothing will be left behind.
> There will lots of boxes all over our house!
> Elizabeth and Ray will put their toys and books into boxes.
> Bunny and Bear will stay with Elizabeth—they do not ride in boxes!
> . . .
> Elizabeth will find her clothes in the boxes and hang them in her new closet.
> She will find her book *Princess, Princess* in a box and put it on the bookshelf.
> Elizabeth, Ray, Mommy, and Daddy will sit down to eat at the old dining table in the new dining room.
> They will be tired and happy.
> The End.

Providing children a visual sequence of what they can expect to happen, using their own names and pictures, figuring out what anxieties they might have, and ending on a good note with something familiar are good strategies that help reduce anxiety and fear. Plus, with a book, or a stapled set of papers to hold and refer to, the child feels a bit more in control.

Social Stories

Scripts and crisis books are very related to social stories in which children are taught ways to appropriately respond. A social story, as originated by Carol Gray (2000), is a structured approach to a social situation that prepares the child for an uncertain event, shares important information, and gives her a strategy to deal with it. In *The New Social Story Book*, Gray defined a social story in this way: "A social story is a short story that describes a situation in terms of relevant social cues and common responses, providing a student with accurate and specific information regarding what occurs in a situation, and why" (p. 1). She often pairs a visual cue with the appropriate response. I personally broke up the process into two steps—providing an action together with a script for memory purposes, and then removing the physical action but adding lots of verbal repetition, because I knew that I couldn't always be there to provide Elizabeth with the visual cue. For example, we would dramatize how to answer a telephone or how to talk to her grandmother. Then, I would verbally remind her of what she could say if the telephone rang and it was her grandmother. We practiced scripts using the context of her real life, and I used the crisis books for events that were outside of a typical day, such as a move or a trip.

Making Things Visual

I have learned to make everything visual to Elizabeth. Luckily for us, this can include language-based things such as lists, but if it's not in front of her so that she can see it, it doesn't get done or understood. She has lists for how to make her own lunch, household chores, morning routines to get out the door, work plans for school, and how to do long division. She will ask, "What's for dinner?" a hundred times until I show her the menu. Baskets in her room are labeled to help her keep things in place. They used to be labeled with pictures, but are now labeled with words. When we recently moved, I had to write out a list for her to keep with her about our itinerary and the schedule we would follow. All of these help with her understanding and help her keep anxiety at bay. I have learned, often the hard way, that when she is melting down, I need to give her room to cool down, and then work up a list or a series of pictures to help her deal with the situation.

Replacement Behaviors

Particularly for the issue of stimming, I quickly learned from research sources, such as the Indiana Resource Center for Autism (2009) and the University of Louisville's Systematic Treatment of Autism & Related Disorders (STAR, 2009) program that the repetitive motions were done to reduce stress or to rebalance for focus. Children can stim during moments of high stress or high joy. The tic or the repetition can ease cortisol levels of anxiety.

Thus, the solution is not to get rid of the stim but to replace it with something that also can help reduce the anxiety. We particularly encountered this with fingernail chewing. Elizabeth's fingernails were bitten down to the quick and would bleed. We tried using nail polish as a reward for not chewing her nails—no success. We tried gentle reminders to stop. No success. Finally, I read about replacement behaviors and tried to get her to press her fingers hard against a surface. That would provide the sensory input that she was wanting and get rid of the "itches" she said she had in her fingers.

Counting

To handle things, I have learned to count them. This was brought home to me by my son's incredibly wise teacher when he was 18 months old. They had indoor activities and outdoor activities, and because we were in Florida, the door between the indoors and outdoors often was open to allow the children to go back and forth. I picked him up from preschool one day and his teacher had "that" look on her face.

"How was Raymond today?" I trepidatiously asked.

"Oh, it was a little tough," she said with a tired smile.

"Oh . . . ?" I asked.

"He really wanted to bring the outdoor trucks and toys inside and we had to keep reminding him that outdoor toys stay outside."

"Oh . . . ?" I asked, feeling there was more to this story than this.

"78 times," she said.

I am truly not exaggerating. The teacher had to "remind" my son *78* times to keep the trucks outside. I was struck by several thoughts:

- What a *patient* teacher—there is no way that I would last 78 times before I lost my temper, cool, whatever.
- The teaching belief of the teacher was not to "correct" him; instead she "reminded" him.
- Often, the secret to kids is just outlasting them. It taught me a coping strategy to being more stubborn than they are: counting!

The next day when I picked him up, I asked how it went that day. The teacher was all smiles and said, "Only 25 times today." This *was* progress!

I have used this counting strategy innumerable times since. We count all kinds of things as a family now. For example, Ray did *not* want to sit down in the bathtub. I placed him in a sitting position 27 times the first day I tried this strategy. The second day was 18, the third 9, and by the fourth day, he had learned that bath time meant sitting down.

We count successes. Elizabeth words grew from 5 at age 2 to 50 by age 2 ½ to beyond counting at age 3. We count how many they got right in the daily multiplication timed test. We count how fast they can get dressed.

I time Raymond's tantrums. The first one, when we were visiting family and he was 2, lasted an hour. The next, when he was 3 at Thanksgiving dinner, lasted an hour and a half. The next, after a move when he was 4, lasted 2 hours, 45 minutes. Full-on, screaming, ranting, hurling-himself-against-walls tantrums. I sobbed through every one of them, and just counted, knowing that they would have to end some time and I would get my son back from the dark place his issues took him to.

I count to let them know how close they are to getting in trouble. "I will count to three, and if you have not gotten quiet/closed the door/gotten off the computer game/stopped annoying your sibling by the time I hit three, you will go to time out/lose privileges/go to bed early . . . " I try my best to make the consequence fit the issue, but I follow one critical rule—I always follow through and I never do things like counting 1,

2, 2 ½, 2 ¾, because I have learned the hard way that children try to see how far past 2 they can push the situation. My children do know that 2 means 2, and that a consequence is coming soon.

Sometimes, just the threat of counting works. My mother was babysitting one night and was getting fed up with them. She gave them her best stern face, and said "One . . . TWO," at which they promptly stopped teasing each other. When my husband and I came home from a rare date together, she laughed that it was a good thing that they stopped because she would have had no idea what to do if she had gotten to three!

Counting helps us all. It lets them know the extent of their behavior. They now ask me to count things for them and they know that Mommy is getting fed up and controlling her own frustration when she starts counting. Counting also provides us all a way of coping. I have learned that counting provides a structure for the children to feel secure within. It is during unsupervised time or lack of rules that both Elizabeth and Ray will get into mischief, whine, or provoke each other until a fight ensues. They like knowing how much time is left in an activity, how far they've pushed my level of tolerance, and how much they've improved.

Writing

Although Ray has fine motor issues, and the children are still young, we are encouraging them to use writing as a means of communicating. It is a strategy that is highly effective in my family, both immediate and extended. When we are uncomfortable, or have to deal with challenging issues, rather than retreating (always a preferred option), we write. E-mail and texting have been saving graces for us, as we have become much more communicative with each other. Any form of confrontation: personal, business, friendly or not, is difficult for us.

However, it goes beyond the emotional aspect of confrontation. There are times that I don't know what I feel until I write it down. Emotions can be such a cascading tidal wave that to process them requires time. Making it visual and seeing it on paper allows us to better identify our emotions and communicate them clearly. It's a characteristic of the spectrum that I recognize in myself and other members of my family. I well remember a "fight" James and I had over the course of several hours as we sent first furious, then huffy, then problem-focused, and finally conciliatory texts to each other. The texts gave us space to deal with things and an opportunity to identify and work toward communication, rather than completely shutting down. James and I flirted and courted over e-mail and it's a medium we still go back to. I am starting to encourage my children to sit down at the computer and write to whoever it is that has upset them. My son has fine motor difficulties, and so we're still working on typing skills, but it's a very specific strategy that I offer them.

Writing it out also is a strategy strongly supported by research. According to Joshua Smyth and Danielle Arigo in the March 2009 edition of the journal *Current Opinion in Psychiatry*, expressive writing and other school-based therapies showed significant ability to help children learn to regulate their emotional outbursts. Such use of writing allows the tension to be released without directly impacting others.

Intellectualizing

One of the original defense mechanisms suggested by Freud, intellectualization is the avoidance of stressful emotions by focusing on fact and logic. Many of the strategies I've described encompass this idea, but with intellectualizing there is an added effort to make things intellectual, rather than emotional. Because they are such passionate, tender little souls with strong cognitive abilities, my children will scream out their frustrations, anger, or even enjoyment of things. They shut down when there is any suggestion of change or emotional judgment. To help with all of these issues, we will ask them to examine the impact of their behavior, before we tell them how to change their behavior. "Elizabeth, how are people reacting to your screaming? I know that you're having a good time, but is there something else you can do that won't scare other people? Ray, how do you think Max felt when you screamed at him? What do you think you could have done differently?"

Such intellectualizing as a coping mechanism is rooted in research dating back to Freud's original psychological studies. When children are taught intellectualizing skills, Dandoy and Goldstein (1990) found that the biological reactions of stress decreased; people were better able to handle their emotional outburst to a stressful situation. In their book, *The Regulation of Emotion*, Pierre Philippot and Robert Stephen Feldman (2008) discussed the process of living an authentically emotionally healthy life, being able to function within society's guidelines for emotional outbursts, and not allowing stress and anxiety rob a person of his ability to function.

The use of intellectualizing questions is not designed to stifle children's emotional development, but to give them space in which to work out their emotions. It also is a process of teaching and reinforcing theory of mind—to help children understand that there are different ways of perceiving things. Because children with high-functioning autism have cognitive abilities that are impacted by autism, they have the ability to learn the sequential steps of taking another's perspective. I also want to give them a feeling of control over the situation by their being able to control their own behavior, rather than fighting me or someone else for that control. It's hard to not react and tell them what to do, and it's hard for them to think about other people's perspectives, but progress is progress, even when it's slow.

Whatever you do, do it thoroughly. None of these various therapies work half-heartedly. Give it time to work. On the other hand, if a treatment is going to be effective, you will see changes within a few weeks. Just because something worked for your neighbor's child doesn't necessarily mean that it will work for yours. Be willing to let go of something if it's not working. And other parents who tell you that you're doing your child harm aren't in your shoes. They don't know the balance that you are trying to maintain between "normal" and "fixing," "curing" and "treating," "my child with autism" and "the rest of my family," and "living" and "being." And remember that your child is ultimately becoming who she is. In his book *Not Even Wrong*, Paul Collins (2005) wrote, "Autistics are the ultimate square pegs, and the problem with pounding a square peg in a round hole is not that the hammering is hard work. It's that you are destroying the peg" (p. 225). It is hard to balance fixing your child and developing your child. To use the old quote, parenting is the hardest job you'll ever love. And parenting a child with autism is the hardest thing you'll ever do—and the most rewarding.

Education—Joining the Highway

5

Schooling is one of the most problematic areas for children with autism. Although the rates of autism have skyrocketed, schools have been unable to keep up. And this is not an issue isolated to the United States. A 2000 study of schools in Wales and Scotland, published by Judith Barnard and colleagues at the National Autistic Society, found that these countries' teachers and schools were woefully underprepared for the numbers of students with autism. Such issues of underpreparedness of teachers are clearly present in the United States as well. And yet, we turn over our children to other people that we trust to love our children, implement the best therapies, listen to us, make accommodations for our children, develop their abilities, and to tell us how things are going.

Trusting educators is a process, and the more that you know, the better able you will be to facilitate the communication.

MONTESSORI EDUCATION

Let me be *very* clear: Montessori education is *not* set up for kids with severe disabilities. They do not ever claim to be an effective intervention, and often do not have special services for children with autism, high-functioning or not. However, originally created for the "lost children" of poverty and neglect, Montessori education follows the child in her own developmental growth. This means that it allows children to progress at their own rate, with a system based on the concept that children will watch first, then try and then master. For my child who was bright, not talking, and watched people before interacting with them, I decided that Montessori education was the perfect thing for her. And it was. I credit our Montessori school with so much of her progress.

To begin with, Montessorians do not ever lock a child into a particular academic or social expectation and the needs of each child are looked at from an individual perspective. Knowing that Elizabeth had language problems when she turned 2, I immediately enrolled her in our local Montessori Toddler program, designed for children aged 18 months to 3 years old. I wanted her around typical children because she watched other children so intensely. I also wanted her in an environment that would not pressure her to join the group, but allow her to watch and try new tasks at her own rate. And lastly, their program is so tactile and hands-on in nature that I knew it would be a great way to gently acclimate her to sensory things. By learning to polish shoes, for example, she would be learning how to handle slippery things.

When she was 2 ½, the teacher of the Infant/Toddler program suggested to me that she be moved up into the Early Childhood classroom for children who were ages 3–5. She was *not* doing the tasks of that age, but as they said to me, and I am eternally grateful to them for this, "She needs to be surrounded by language, and the kids in that age group have higher language levels than the toddlers." I did *not* suggest this movement, and was amazed that her teachers would suggest something that was outside the "rules" to meet the needs of my child. This truly was an outstanding school that looked at each child as an individual and focused on meeting those needs. It's an ideal you rarely see.

It was one we paid for, though. Montessori schools, especially private ones, tend to be expensive, but I know that teaching her to talk and be social was worth every penny of it. My daughter is now two grade levels ahead in reading and three in math, and I credit the individual approach her teachers took in her educational process to this gain.

It is worthwhile noting that the word "Montessori" is in the public domain, which means that *any* school can call itself a "Montessori school" regardless of teacher training or beliefs. I would encourage parents, if Montessori education looks appealing, to make sure that the school is accredited by either one of the Montessori accrediting agencies and that the teachers have received Montessori training from a Montessori-accredited teacher preparation program. Such training and accreditations are more likely to ensure that the school is committed to accepting individual differences and to developing the abilities of its students.

PRIVATE EDUCATION

There are a whole host of private schools that specialize, and claim to specialize, in working with children with autism. There are 800,000 sites that describe private placement and autism on Google, so there certainly are a large number of choices. Good ones, however, are more difficult to find.

Private schools, in general, are under no legal obligation to educate children with autism. If your child has a label, no matter how high functioning he or she is, private schools have the right to deny you services, based on the premise that they cannot meet the diverse needs of your child. However, labels are not public knowledge. But you do need to think before you enroll your child in a program without disclosing his issues. A friend of mine works in a private school and shares how parents try to "sneak" their children in. It almost always backfires, particularly when the child is having a meltdown or a bad day. Difference looks different, and teachers are experts at knowing what level of difference their school can tolerate. I found that it was better to describe Elizabeth's symptoms, but steer away from the label that has so much baggage associated with it. I brought in IQ and achievement test scores to back up my claim that she was "very smart but learned differently," and noted that she had sensory issues and that while her language is strong, teachers have to give her time to respond. I relied on her testing data to communicate with teachers, not the label. Private schools are a mixed bag—they can be very, very good, or very, very bad.

There are other private schools that specialize in children with disabilities, but most of them do not accept children with autism, and often are significantly confused about children with high-functioning autism. They tend to be designed for children with typical social skills, but poor reading skills. Autism is perceived as such a high-needs area and so specialized that most private schools are not willing to take on the behavioral and learning needs of children whose needs are literally all over the spectrum. The perception among educators is that children with autism are harder to teach, and that generalization may or may not be applicable to an individual child.

Lastly, there are private schools who accept only children with autism. And here is one of the biggest dilemmas parents face. Because they only take children with autism, there will be only children with autism for your child to be around. Similarly, these schools are used to a population that often is severely cognitively impaired. There will be few role models, but there should be a staff who is caring and understands the complexities of autism and who are more likely to communicate and work with you. Such skilled expertise can be expensive. Schools can commonly be $50,000 a year and upward. And public schools generally are unwilling to pay the cost of private school placement because these are the most restrictive placements possible.

Children who do best in these placements tend to have either such severe autism that the impact of peers is negligible, or they have faced such extreme teasing and abuse in a more inclusive setting that they're deeply unhappy. In a school for children with autism, everyone understands autism and the child is more able to be his own person, free from the expectations of the label.

Another issue in private school settings is that there tends to be tremendous turnover rate among staff. Most private schools do not pay teachers what public schools can. Teachers at private schools often are there to get their first years of teaching down, and then are drawn away by the public system, or have retired from the public system and are supplementing their income until they "really" retire. Because stability and routine are so important to children with autism, losing a favorite teacher can be truly traumatic. Also, the effectiveness of the interventions may be based on the training of the individual teacher.

Perhaps one of your better options, if your child is strong enough to compete academically, is a private school for children with gifts and talents. They are used to children having diverse academic abilities, and many of their children have social challenges as well, so they are well-prepared to work with children with diverse needs. However, instruction and interaction in a school for gifted children tends to be highly auditory and language-based. Most children who attend a school for gifted children are very fluent in language and make jokes and puns that may be beyond your child's abilities. In addition, your child's visual needs or language challenges may not be appropriately met here. You will need to balance many factors when considering schooling.

If you are checking out private school options, be sure to ask some of the following questions:

- Are you licensed? Licensing means that they have to meet certain health code and operating requirements.
- Are you accredited? Accreditation means that an outside agency is holding them accountable for meeting their goals and for operating in a certain manner. No accreditation means that anyone with any agenda can open up a school.
- Are your teachers licensed and by whom? What percentage are credentialed?
- What is your retention rate among teachers and staff? Among students and families?
- What is your approach to discipline? Do you use restraint, time out, or behavior modification?
- What is your approach to education? What philosophy or treatment style do you use? What is your emphasis? Academic skills? Social skills? Functional skills?
- What role do you see the parents playing in your school? How do you want us to be involved?
- How and how often do you evaluate student progress?
- How do you communicate with parents and how often? What kinds of formal and informal communication strategies do you use? What can I expect to hear from my child's teacher on a regular basis? What kinds of communication do you expect from parents?
- Is there a learning or behavioral specialist on the team?
- What other supports do you offer, such as occupational therapy, speech therapy, or art therapy?
- Do you offer any special classes such as art, music, PE, or sports?
- When students leave your program, where do they generally go? What forms of support do you provide for this transitional period?

You should have an idea of what answers you want to hear from them. You will rarely, if ever, get all of the right answers from the same place. The goal is optimization—the highest number of the best answers from one place. There may be a place that does one thing exactly the way you like it. Weigh that in consideration with the other issues and make the best determination you can.

And be prepared to change. Schools can say one thing, and do something completely different. I knew a school that had the greatest person selling the school. She verbalized exactly what we were looking for, seemed to be in alignment with my philosophy, and I sent my children off, content that they were being taken care of and cared for. In reality, the principal had little follow through and poor communication with her staff. My children had a great teacher, but when she left, we left.

HOMESCHOOLING

For parents who cannot find a system that works for them, or who perceive that no one else has the specific knowledge of what works for their child, homeschooling is an option that is growing rapidly in popularity. There is a significant financial element because it generally requires the full-time involvement of at least one parent, as well as training costs for the parent who is providing the educational interventions. Hidden costs come in as well as you provide social engagement opportunities for your child. Camps and sports activities where children can meet and engage with other children cost money because they aren't provided through the school. It also can put stress on a marriage when one parent is providing direct treatment, and the other is not.

However, the education is absolutely tailor-made to your child. If your child is obsessed with cars, then math, reading, and history instruction all can focus around cars. If the child has an attentional issue one day, you can back off. If he's interested in one thing all day, you can adapt to that as well. The parent understands what can motivate and move a child forward. Also, because homeschooling is such a growing movement, there are thousands of websites dedicated to curriculum and activities for children that the parent can access. Also, most larger communities will offer social activities and connections to other homeschooling parents. Our local sports facility offers homeschool swim classes during the day for families to interact with each other, and local museums will offer field trip opportunities for homeschooling families.

Each state will have different requirements for the homeschooling process. Some of them will require extensive daily logs, testing, and portfolios. Others will require that you check in every now and then. Research the laws, and join your state's homeschool organization to advocate for needed changes. When done poorly, homeschooled children can suffer significant neglect. However, when done well, homeschooling can be a fantastic experience for the child and the parent.

SPECIAL EDUCATION

As I have mentioned before, I was thrilled with the intensive therapy provided by Early Intervention. I cannot say the same for the services from the public schools once Elizabeth turned 3. At 3, she moved from EI to special education within our local school district. I was so annoyed that the group who had gotten to know her so well would be cast off and there would be no follow-up possible.

At her Individualized Education Program (IEP) meeting, we went over goals: Yes, Elizabeth would be using age-level language skills. Yes, she would be interacting with other children to learn how to ask for things. All good. Then, they turned to me and said, "We have two options for services. The first is a full-day self-contained program for children with autism and the second is a part-time self-contained program for children with autism." I was livid!

Elizabeth, then and now, is a mimic of behavior. She tries so hard to figure out the code of social acceptance that she will watch everyone around her and act in that manner. If things were calm, Elizabeth was calm. If things were chaotic, Elizabeth was in the middle of it. The *last* thing my mimic daughter needed was to be in a self-contained classroom of other children with autistic behaviors. Hers would only get worse! She had been in a Montessori classroom with typical peers and had been doing very well.

"Can't she get services that were deemed to be necessary and appropriate just a week before?" Well, no, sorry. The school system didn't offer that. Sometimes, they did have kids from neighboring preschools come and play with the kids in a structured environment. This, *this* was inclusion?

"What about the therapy?"

"Well, that's in a group setting."

Soooo, let me get this straight. She's moving from personalized, individualized, one-on-one services that come to her school to a self-contained program with group therapy and I'm supposed to be OK with this?

Special education is caught in a bind of what is called "free appropriate public education," commonly known as FAPE. "Free" is what it sounds like: Services are to be provided at no cost to families so that money does not play a role in a family's decision. The sticky part is the "appropriate" part. The 1982 Supreme Court case *Board of Education of the Hendrick Hudson Central School District v. Rowley* clarified that appropriate does not mean "best" or "maximizing." It means "appropriate for growth to happen."

What this means for children with high-functioning autism is that schools are required to serve the *disability*, but are not required to serve the child's *strengths*. If a child is managing to function at grade level, even though his abilities may be higher, or there is a significant struggle to do so, no services are federally mandated. In the states that provide gifted education services by state law, advanced services have to be provided for children who are outperforming their peers, but not necessarily for children who have the potential for high performance but aren't achieving to that potential because of a disabling condition.

In our case, I had not a legal leg to stand on if I were unhappy with what they had to offer. Now, in some egregious cases, parents have taken their school districts to court to provide better services for their child and won. That option was not available to us.

I was in a unique situation. The degrees I hold meant that I was treated very, very carefully. I was particularly irritated one day when they set up a meeting close to the time Elizabeth was to turn 3. I assumed that it was a planning meeting to go over options for her treatment. I had to find a babysitter willing to work with my two active and sensitive little ones, plan around my teaching schedule, and go down to the school district's central offices. At this meeting, I was told that that purpose of the meeting was to let me know that a planning meeting would be necessary because Elizabeth was turning 3, and we would no longer be served under Early Intervention, something I had already been told clearly by both the therapists and the Early Intervention people (I also had signed a paper stating that I was aware of these changes). I was so angry that they would waste my time and money scheduling a meeting whose only purpose was to schedule another meeting. But they had to make very sure that they covered themselves legally with me. Because I knew the law (heck, I taught the class!), they were very careful with me. I'm not saying that they weren't this careful with everyone, but I did not feel the gentle helpfulness I had felt with the Early Intervention folks. There was nothing I felt I could do with the school system. I opted out and we decided to go it alone for the next 5 years. Which cost more money . . .

I know that other school districts are not so limited in their choices. There has been so much publicity since then and there have been so many more advances made that many school districts now offer a wide range of services that are appropriate for the diversity found among kids with autism. With the expansion of Early Intervention to age 6, those wonderful services we had now can last for much longer than we were limited to. I can completely understand the dilemma of school districts trying to serve preschool-aged children with disabilities especially when they did not have access to children without disabilities of the same age to create a typical inclusion setting. Elizabeth was just 1 year too old.

Programs of Note

There are other systems that are doing amazing things with autism. Pleasant Grove Elementary, a public school in Indianapolis, IN, has a "wiggle room" in which kids with autism can retreat when they are feeling overwhelmed and need a break before they have an outburst. The CHIME Charter School in Woodland Hills, CA, specializes in inclusive education for children, starting with preschool and going through middle school. There are a number of excellent private schools for children with autism that focus on one type of therapy or another. However, where we lived, none of these were options.

SPECIAL EDUCATION IN PUBLIC SCHOOLS

The following is a synopsis of special education. For more information, please go the National Dissemination Center for Children with Disabilities (http://www.nichcy.org), Wrightslaw (http://www.wrightslaw.com), or the Office of Special Education and Rehabilitative Services through the U.S. Department of Education (http://www.ed.gov/about/offices/list/osers/osep/index.html) websites.

Funding Issues

Public education is free—all of it. If specialized programs, equipment, technology, and services, including people to individually assist your child, are deemed necessary to help your child, all of it is free to you. However, it is important to realize when you are working with the school system that they have to operate under significant financial constraints, and all of their dealings with you will take that into consideration, even though legally, they're not supposed to. Susan Senator (2005) referred to it as the business model of education—not a bad metaphor.

Special education in the public schools is required by federal law, known as the Individuals with Disabilities Education Improvement Act, commonly called IDEA. It is reauthorized by Congress and significant changes are made to it every 7 years. The last version was conducted in 2004, so it's called IDEA 2004. About ⅓, or 33% of the federal education budget is taken up with special education. Because approximately 10%–20% of students in schools are in special education, there is an unequal distribution; it is clear that it is more expensive to educate children with disabilities.

However, all of this federal money only pays for approximately 8% of the actual cost of special education borne by a school district, according to the U.S. Department of Education (2005). The remaining 92% of the monies have to come from the state and the district—most often from the district. IDEA is very close to an unfunded mandate from the federal government: Districts are required to follow very specific procedures and provide specific services, and yet they are given very little money to do so by the federal government. In cases where districts have claimed that they are unable to provide such services because of their economic woes, the Supreme Court has told them that they must—and they must simply take the costs from other operating expenses. Thus, it is in the interest of school systems to keep their special education costs under control, but provide enough services that students benefit.

There is a legal definition of the word "benefit" as well: The education for any one child has to provide a setting in which it is expected that that child will make progress. It is *not* required that the educational experience be maximized for optimal growth of that child, nor purely for social reasons. This means that school districts are always trying to balance what is a "good enough" education for a child and the desires of the parents. When I teach the special education law class, I tell my students that special education has been shaped by court cases, and that while individuals may want to do the best for children, the system has to maximize its public tax dollars for all children. Thus, there is an inherent tension built in between the needs of the school district to provide adequate education for all of their children with the budget that they have and the needs of the parents to have excellent educational opportunities for their child.

This doesn't necessarily mean that the process has to be overtly adversarial, though. Districts and parents are not automatically on opposite sides; in fact, they do have the same goal—to educate the child in the best manner possible and to help her grow. It's just that the word "possible" means different things depending on which side of the table you're sitting on.

IEP vs. 504

All public schools are required to serve all of their students, so special education is designed to work with students who (a) have a disability, *and* (b) have some form of school problem that *only* a change in instruction would address. If there is an adverse effect on educational achievement, but a change in the accessibility to the instruction would address it, students may have a disability, but not qualify for special education.

If this is the case, but they still need some accommodations or modifications in order to perform well in school, parents have the right to ask for a 504 Plan. Section 504 is part of the Rehabilitation Act of 1973 that requires employers to provide equal access to their employees in order to do their jobs; they cannot discriminate, based on the employee's disability and the employer's requirement to provide access. For example, if your office is on the second floor, you are not allowed to deny a person in a wheelchair a job if he is capable of doing the job once he has access to the office. The employer has to provide ramps or elevators or some form of access. If you think of children with disabilities as employees, they have the right to access the traditional school curriculum and not have their disability get in the way of that access. Schools have to make accommodations. A 504 Plan is where the school, the parents, and sometimes the child plan what kinds of accommodations are needed to access the regular curriculum. Students on a 504 Plan do not need specialized instruction, but they may need more frequent breaks, or opportunity to move around more, or even special equipment. My children, because they are on grade level for their academic work, but might need accommodations in order to remain there, would be served under a 504 Plan.

A 504 Plan protects both the district and the child. An individual, fabulous teacher might make some classroom accommodations for a child—allowing him to get up out of his seat or giving him extended time for projects and tests. But if the child moves to a teacher the next year who is more inflexible, a 504 Plan will *require* that teacher to make specific changes to her classroom. She does not have to change the curriculum, but she will be required to change how she instructs, based on the specific needs of the child. And the district is protected by a 504 Plan, because it documents that it is not discriminating against a child with a disability while providing access to the curriculum. There are fewer parental rights under a 504 Plan than there are under an IEP. However, parents do have the right to call a 504 Plan meeting at any time to review its effectiveness, request additional assessments, and so forth.

If a child qualifies for a disability, *and* it is determined that she needs particular services in order to progress, an IEP will be written. An IEP spells out what the educational plan is for *that* child, based upon her strengths and areas of challenge. They are not supposed to be "cookie cutter" plans in which every child in a classroom is working on the same goal. They are supposed to be specific to the child and followed by every teacher and professional within that school. It is a document full of legal protections for the child and the parents that specific steps will be followed, or there will be legal repercussions.

Such repercussions are rare. Although the IEP process often is based upon an adversarial relationship, rather than a collaborative one, the implementation of the plan requires collaboration efforts in which both schools and parents must engage. It is in the best interests of everyone to collaborate and work together to create a positive educational experience for a child.

Special Education Processes

Getting to an IEP often is a long and frustrating process firmly established by federal law. However, there are small, but significant differences between states and districts in the way they translate the law. You will need to check out the specific processes for your individual state. Essentially, there are seven steps:

- *Initial Problem*: The child is observed by the classroom teacher to have difficulties or problems in school. Problems can be academic, behavioral, or social. Or, the parents can bring the plight of the child to the attention of the team, sometimes called a Student Support Team (SST) or prereferral team.

- *Prereferral Team*: The teacher (or the parents) brings the name of the child to the team with a description of the problem. The team generally is a group of general educators, with some limited participation by special education professionals. The parents are rarely directly involved at this point, but do have the right to be there, and are notified of the team's decisions. The team then makes recommendations that can be implemented relatively quickly as well as any screening assessments that might be done by teachers. In a school system that is following Response to Intervention (RTI), these recommendations have to be carefully documented and based on research. A waiting period of about 6–9 weeks generally is recommended to give the strategies time to work and for documentation to be gathered to determine their effectiveness.

- *Referral Team*: Once the data of the prereferral team have been gathered, the referral team will make a decision whether to move forward. If the strategies were effective in bringing about changes in the child, then it is decided that there probably wasn't a disability—it was just a gap in the learning process or a mismatch between the educational environment and the child's learning style. However, if little to no progress has occurred, the team can make an official recommendation for formal assessment. Parental permission is required, and generally, the school's psychologists become involved. In more progressive school districts, special educators and school psychologists are involved early in the process. In some states, they are prohibited from doing so. It is important to note that when a parent insists on assessment or when a child comes to a district with an already-diagnosed disability that has already received services, such as autism, most school districts move directly to the assessment step.

- *Assessment*: The purpose of the assessment process is to determine the nature of an educational problem, whether it is academic, behavioral, or social. Assessments can be tests, observations, interviews, or checklists. Often schools use a multidisciplinary assessment that explores all of the needs of the child within a school environment. Your child may have a fully developed autism diagnosis, but the school will still need to do a thorough assessment for educational purposes. Once the assessment is completed, there has to be an eligibility meeting.

- *Eligibility*: Required by federal law to be held within 60 days of the parent's written consent to formal assessment recommendation (the definition of days as calendar days, school days, or business days is up to the state; and if a parent never formally signs consent on paper, the timeline has not started), the IEP eligibility meeting determines if the child meets the educational definition of disability. Each state has a slightly different version of its eligibility requirements. You will need to check with your own state to see if it follows federal suggestions, the *DSM-IV* guidelines for autism as delineated by the American Psychiatric Association (2000), or its own. I laugh with my students, with no real sense of humor about it, that the best way to "cure" some disabilities is to move. It also is important to know that there is a difference between an "educational definition" and a "medical definition" of a disability. This distinction is most commonly seen in the issue of dyslexia, which is a more medical/psychological term for great reading difficulties. Dyslexia can fall under the educational term of "specific learning disability," but it doesn't always. A child might meet the definition of dyslexia provided by a private psychologist, but not meet the definition for learning disability. Although somewhat historically rare for children with autism, there are a growing number of cases where a school system has denied services because the child doesn't meet the educational definition of autism. If this is the case, the parent needs to get a written copy of what the state's educational definition of autism is, because the federal suggestions mirror medical guidelines. However, some have placed more restrictions on its autism label, excluding some of the more higher functioning children. This was our issue: When we moved, Elizabeth qualified under medical guidelines, but not under educational ones. And there wasn't a darn thing we could do about it unless we wanted a fight.

- *Need for Services*: This decision usually is conducted at the eligibility meeting, but it is a federally defined separate decision process. The team then decides if the child not only meets the definitional test, but also needs specially designed instruction in order to benefit from schooling. If the child has a disability, but does not need specialized services, she may be eligible for a 504 Plan. But if she *does* need specially designed instruction (SDI), she is to receive an IEP.

- *IEP Meeting*: Generally immediately after the need for services decision, but not always, an IEP is written if the child was found eligible for special education. In the next section, I detail the parts of an IEP, but it should be emphasized that the IEP is written by the team; it should never be the sole creation of a single person—teacher, therapist, or parent. Although most teachers and schools may come in with a draft of goals written ahead of time, all of them are up for discussion and negotiation. The IEP spells out what it is that the schools are going to do for your child, and it is an agreement regarding the services and programs that will be provided. Schools *must* provide the services, programs, and accommodations that are listed on the child's IEP.

Rights Under IDEA

There are several basic assumptions that IDEA is founded on. These all translate into specific parental rights. These include:

- Zero Reject: No child, no matter how profoundly disabled, can be denied educational services. This does not guarantee all children rights to the *same* educational experiences, but all children have the basic right to an education that is appropriate for them.
- Free Appropriate Public Education (FAPE): This is the underlying assumption of the law. According to the Learning Disabilities Association of America (2004):

  - Free requires that the education of each child with a disability be provided at public expense and at no cost to the child's parents. The only exception is that incidental fees normally charged to nondisabled students or their parents as part of the regular education program also may be charged to students with disabilities and their parents.
  - Appropriate means that each child with a disability is entitled to an education that is appropriate for his or her needs. Appropriate education is determined on an individual basis and may not be the same for each child with a disability.
  - Public refers to the public school system. Children with disabilities, regardless of the nature or severity of their disabilities, have the same right to attend public schools as their nondisabled peers. The public school system must educate students with disabilities, respond to their individual needs, and help them plan for their future. Private schools are not held to the same requirements to provide services as the public schools.
  - IDEA is an education act that guarantees that eligible children with disabilities will receive a public education that includes

special education and related services as directed by the child's IEP, based on the child's individual needs. (para. 3)

- Assessment shall be given in the child's strongest language, if English is not his first language. This is to make sure that English language learners are not found to be poorly performing because they were tested in English, rather than their native language. However, if these students perform more strongly in English than their native language, they can be evaluated in English.

- Districts must follow due process, which means that they must follow the rules that they set for themselves. If they do not, the parents can hold them liable. If schools state that they operate within a time frame, they must follow that time frame. If they state that they have to communicate in writing, they have to communicate in writing. Parents and school districts might disagree, but if the school districts did not follow due process, they have no hope of winning if legal repercussions are brought against them.

- In the law, Congress states that one goal of IDEA 2004 is " . . . strengthening the role and responsibility of parents and ensuring that families of such children have meaningful opportunities to participate in the education of their children at home and at school" (20 U.S.C. 1400 (c)). In other words, the school district *must* make an attempt to include parents at every step along the way.

- Children with disabilities have the right to be educated to the greatest extent possible with their nondisabled peers in the Least Restrictive Environment (LRE). This means that separate classes, programs, schools, or other removal of children with disabilities from the regular education environment occurs only when the nature or severity of the disability is such that education in regular classes with the use of supplementary aids and services cannot be achieved satisfactorily. If schools are to provide separate experiences, they must justify such placement.

- After reviewing the educational data available, the IEP committee must design special educational instruction to meet the unique needs of the child with a disability, coupled with any additional related services that are required to assist a child with a disability to benefit from that instruction.

Other Parental and Family Rights

Before you go into any official meeting, it helps to know what you have the right to ask. For more complete lists of parent rights, please go to your state's special education regulations, or http://www.wrightslaw. com. The website has an excellent description of the various laws and application to parents. You have the right to:

- Be present at all school meetings about your child. The school can hold the initial set of meetings without you, but you must be invited to the eligibility, determination of need, and IEP meetings in writing.
- Bring anyone else you want to any of the meetings. I have been a parent advocate at numerous meetings because I speak "educationalese" and can facilitate the process for them. Know that if you do bring in an advocate, you might put the district on the defensive, because the presence of an advocate can be the first step in a lawsuit and the focus of the meeting can shift away from meeting the needs of your child to the district covering its legal bases. However, you also can play the roles of "good cop/bad cop" and let the advocate do all of the demanding, while you do most of the accommodating.
- Give or refuse assessment of your child. If you want your child assessed by the school district, that permission must be granted in writing.
- Have an independent educational evaluation (IEE) that has to be considered in addition to the data provided by the school-based assessment team. Parents have the right to have this information, but they might have to pay for an IEE themselves. For example, the school might find that a student does not meet eligibility based on the evaluation results. However, an independent psychologist might

very well find different results. Schools have to take both sets of data into consideration.

- Ask for mediation, an impartial due process hearing, if you are not pleased with the process or the outcomes of the meetings. Mediation is designed to avoid a court case if possible. Parents and the school both have the right to request mediation and then move to a court case if the decision in mediation is not acceptable. However, if you request a court case and lose, you may be required to pay the court costs.

- Inspect and review your child's educational records.

- Be given written prior notice on matters regarding the identification, evaluation, or educational placement of your child.

- Be given a full explanation of all of the procedural safeguards. You also can ask questions about what the jargon means.

- Appeal the initial hearing decision to the State Education Agency (SEA) if the SEA did not conduct the hearing (the school district has the right to do this as well).

- Have the child remain in his or her present educational placement, unless the parent and the school agree otherwise, while administrative or judicial proceedings are pending.

- Participate in, and appeal if necessary, discipline decisions regarding your child.

- Call an IEP meeting, even if it is not the scheduled time, to address concerns or changes that have occurred.

- Receive special education services until the child is 21 or until he or she graduates high school with a regular diploma, whichever comes first.

Writing a Good IEP

The IEP is made up of several interrelated and significant parts. These include:

- *Present Levels of Performance or Present Levels of Educational Performance (PLOP or PLEP)*: These statements summarize any testing data that is present on the child and any documented progress or changes in the child. PLOP can include information on a child's behavior, academic levels, or social/emotional states. They also include statements of student strength and areas in which the child is making growth. These statements of performance must then directly lead to the child's goals. There cannot be a goal written unless there is documentation that such a need exists in the PLOP.

- *Annual Goals*: Must be measurable and objective. They should be as specific as possible. This means that vague, fuzzy terms like "appreciate" or "understand" should not be used. Even fuzzier goals like "improve social interactions" should be made much more specific. IDEA 2004 took away the short-term objectives that may have guided schools in their determination of progress. I teach my students to follow a "formula" for goal writing—ABCD:
  - Antecedent: under what circumstances?: "Given a third-grade-level book SWBAT (Student Will Be Able To) . . ."
  - Behavior: the verb involved: "Describe"
  - Condition: what it is that the child is working with: "the plot of the story"
  - Determinant: the degree to which he should master the skill or behavior *and* how it is to be measured: "at a Proficient level, as determined by the classroom teacher." Some examples include:
    - In the classroom, Elizabeth will be able to maintain eye contact with her teacher and familiar peers 50% of the time, as based on observations by the school psychologist.
    - On the playground, Ray will be able to play with one or two age peers for a period of 15 minutes with sustained attention, as determined by classroom teacher observation.
    - Given a math test, Brandon will be able to multiply two digit numbers with carrying, 90% of the time, as determined by classroom work.

- *Program Provided or Special Education Services Provided*: The IEP team will have to describe how long the services should be provided, and where they are to take place, keeping in mind the need for the Least Restrictive Environment. Similarly, the amount of time that the child will interact in the general education program also must be specified. Some districts have a more inclusive approach than others. Inclusion, simply defined, is the concept that rather than having the student move to the special services, the services come to the child. The child tends to stay in the general education classroom, and special education teachers and other specialists come into the classroom to provide direct services to the child. Generally, teachers collaborate, coteach, and plan activities together that allow the child to participate as fully as possible in the general education curriculum. However, there may be many variations of this model in a school. Other districts may rely more on a continuum of services model in which students might go to a resource room for a smaller student-teacher ratio during specified periods of time. Or, students might be in a self-contained class, or even a special school. You will have to decide which approach is more important to you.

- *Related Services Provided and Length of Time Provided*: All of the services, such as occupational therapy, speech therapy, and adaptive physical education, and the length of time that service is to be provided have to be specified. Sometimes, this is provided in minutes over the course of a week or a month. The longer the time frame, the more likely it is that the school may not be providing exact amounts of service per week. You should ask for it in terms of the smallest increments you can get the team to agree on. How long each day does your child get to see the specialist? Once a day for 15 minutes might be more effective than twice a week for 30 minutes, or 120 minutes each month. You will have to decide this as a team. But you can certainly always ask for as much service as you feel would be beneficial!

- *Modifications and Accommodations*: These are the changes that are necessary within a classroom that will allow the child access to the general education curriculum; modifications are changes in the standards, while accommodations do not require changes in the general education curriculum. They generally inform the teacher of the changes she will need to make, such as preferential seating, allowing frequent breaks, extended time on tests, or a scribe to write for a child. This section also can include various forms of technology that may need to be present to help the child communicate, such as a Picture Exchange Communication System (PECS) or a computer with vocal abilities.

- *Means and Frequency of Communicating to Parents*: A report documenting a student's progress toward his goals has to be specified in the IEP. Often, this is on the same schedule as other students' report cards. However, you can request more frequent communication if there is a new therapy or strategy you're trying at home. Also, the assessments and methods of evaluation toward the accomplishment of the goals must be specified. Schools are required to collect, monitor, and analyze IEP progress data throughout the IEP timeline. Parents can ask to review samples of evidence to ensure that the regular reports are not simply a hunch or unspecified observation but rather a systematic process designed to ensure that the Specially Designed Instruction is working or not. This is particularly important for students with autism.

- *Testing Accommodations (if any)*: When students are given high-stakes tests that determine their progression to the next grade, or the school's overall performance on its goals, some students are allowed to receive alternative tests. However, such alternatives are limited by the state to around 2% of the population and generally are given to students with more profound disabilities. If you have concerns with the administration of inappropriate tests, you should talk to your school test administrator about this. However, administration of these tests can be modified, such as allowing the test to be given in a smaller environment or read aloud.

- *Time Frame of the IEP*: Generally, IEPS are good for a year, but IDEA 2004 allowed states to choose to do 3-year IEPs if parents agree in writing. Most states still require an annual IEP review and meeting to write new goals for the next year, but some are considering moving to a more flexible, long-term format.

- *Statement of Transition*: By the time the child is at least 16 years old, although some states require it at the age of 14, the IEP team must start thinking about the goals of the family and child after high school. Adult services start getting involved at this time so that the movement from school placement to adult living is as smooth as possible.

Professional Boundaries

What is notable because it is missing are the specifications of educational approaches or therapies. Rarely do IEPs tell teachers and therapists how to do their jobs; they just specify what they are to have accomplished at the end of it. It assumes that teachers are professional enough to be able to select the most effective instructional approach and do not require additional teacher training. However, if you have a particular therapy program that you have been using that has been successful, you can request that it be put into the IEP. You may not get very far with that, and there is no legal right given to you to require it, but you certainly can ask. It can be very confusing to a child to switch from one therapy program one year to a different one the next year, so you should emphasize the educational, behavioral, and social impact of such changes.

Getting the Most Out of Your IEP Team

Realize that an IEP meeting is a negotiation. It is in everyone's best interest to collaborate and provide a plan for your child's educational experience that helps the child. There are a number of things that you can do to help facilitate this process.

Attitudes

Believe that the teachers and administrators involved ultimately have your child's best interests at heart also. They may have different rules and different expectations, but they are in the profession of helping children.

Recognize different areas of expertise. You are the expert for your child and you will have a better idea than anyone about what might and might not work for your child. However, the professionals involved have been trained in disabilities and may have expertise in a process of education that you do not. The IEP meeting is an excellent way to match your child's needs with the variety of strategies that the district can offer. You both can learn from each other.

Be prepared to be very firm on some things and to allow the education professionals some leeway as well. Be ready to give in and to insist. Also be prepared for "happy talk" that says very little. "Elizabeth is delightful" makes everyone feel good, but it is not useful in order to write a goal. "Elizabeth should be provided puzzles in order to strengthen her spatial abilities" is more specific and practical.

Relatedly, be ready to insist on the school addressing your child's strengths as well. An IEP meeting is designed to meet the needs of the whole child, which can include areas of strength. These strengths just have to be documented and stated in the PLOP. Most people tend to focus on the "can'ts," but the IEP also should focus on the "cans."

Also be prepared for private matters to be discussed. Your child's potty training history, who lives with you, and the relationship you might have with your child's father (or mother) are all relevant information to your child's educational progress.

Before the Meeting

Be prepared. Come early, and have all of your child's documentation. Plan through what you would like to see happen at the IEP meeting. Familiarize yourself with the format of the IEP form so that you can more easily discuss it. Have some draft goals you might like to see happen.

You also should familiarize yourself with your child's testing and evaluation data before the meeting. You have the right to see it ahead of time, so consider requesting this well in advance of the meeting. It can be beneficial to ask if you can meet your child's teachers and therapists ahead of time, and you should visit the new school or classroom if possible.

During the Meeting

Take thorough notes. Ask those speaking to slow down if you need them to. Document any disagreements in writing.

Make sure that the goals being set for your child are challenging, yet realistic. If you get upset about the team's decision, you can ask for a moment to calm yourself down before discussing it further. Most members of the team will understand.

During the meeting you should feel comfortable speaking up even if you're not asked a direct question. Often, the school professionals will outnumber you and they are very familiar with each other and the process, so there is a tendency to steamroll right over the parent. Insist on being heard. Don't allow yourself to be bullied, but also don't be a bully. Just maintain as calm an outlook as possible.

At the same time, you want to listen very carefully to what is being said. Teachers and administrators often are not able to say things that you are, but they can delicately suggest to the parent what is possible. For example, when I was a teacher, I could not suggest that children be evaluated with a nonverbal IQ test, because that would make the school district liable for the cost of the evaluation and it was something that was outside the normal evaluation process. But I *could* say, "Do you have any nonverbal IQ information for your child?" Most parents don't know about the existence or power of a nonverbal IQ test. Similarly, when I was a teacher, I used to carefully explain their rights to parents when I felt that the district was taking advantage of them. I couldn't tell parents what to do, because my job would be in jeopardy, but I could let them know they could do something. If you have a sympathetic teacher with whom you've established a relationship, listen very carefully to what he or she "really" might be saying.

If your child is not present, communicate his or her fears about the process to the team. If there will be changes, you can share probable reactions of your child. If your child is present, be sure to facilitate the child's communication with the team. Help members of the team speak to your child, and help your child speak with them. Be sure to redirect some questions that you know that your child can answer. You are an advocate for your child and representing him as well as yourself at the IEP meeting.

Remember that if you have any questions about the IEP, you can take a few days to sign it. You do not have to sign it right then and there and you should not feel pressured to do so. However, even if you do sign the paperwork, you are not necessarily agreeing with the conclusions of the IEP team. You have the right to convene the team again if you have concerns or questions.

After the IEP Meeting: Working With Your Child's Teachers

Perhaps the best thing you can do for your child is to become involved with and reinforce her experiences at school. If you and your child's teachers are on the same page, your child can make tremendous progress.

Here are some strategies for working well with your child's teacher. You can find more online, but in general:

- Give your child's teacher some time to get to know your child. The beginning of any school year is a crazy time for all teachers. Give everyone time to settle into a normal routine before you appear on the scene. You should try to give the teacher at least 2 weeks before you make an appointment to talk to him.
- Introduce yourself and share something positive about the teacher that you've learned. You might have to really reach, but generally there will be something (ask your child if there is anything in particular

he really likes about his teacher or what he is learning—this usually is helpful when building compliments).

- State that you would like to reinforce the activities and strategies that are taking place within the classroom. Ask him to share some of the activities or ideas for parents with you. Let him know that you are a fellow team member and that you are willing to help as well.

- Offer some specific help to the teacher. For example, you can offer to read to a small group of children every Friday afternoon. The parent I had the best working relationship with offered to help with art activities every Monday at 1 p.m. If you have a skill of your own, offer to share it with her. If you can write, draw, or even weave, offer to teach the children. If you can't be in the classroom, offer to help with the newsletter or to contact other parents for activities. There is a tremendous amount of work that can be done to help the teacher!

- If your first interaction with a teacher is a negative one in which she is calling to complain about your child's behavior, you should listen carefully, and validate the teacher's anger or frustration. Then, you can make suggestions that you have found helpful from other teachers or situations. You also should state that you would like to check in with the teacher within the week to see if the strategies you suggested are effective.

- If something changes in your home environment, you should communicate that to the teacher that day if possible. You don't want the teacher to think that changes in your child's behavior are due to the effectiveness of the strategies, and you want the teacher to be proactive and avoid escalating things if your child is already fragile.

- Offer to design a form that can be quickly used that lists your child's IEP goals and activities associated with them. When I was a teacher, I had a checklist for each child that listed IEP goals and every day I documented which goals we worked on. If the teacher doesn't do that, the creation of a form can be a real headache. Offer to help with various paperwork regarding your child.

- If your child has a teacher who is difficult, poorly trained, or overwhelmed, be sympathetic and offer suggestions that you have found helpful. Give the relationship between the two of you some time to work. Also realize that even though *you* may not like the teacher, the key thing to focus on is your child's relationship and progress. We had a teacher for my son that I found to be incredibly brusque and rude to parents. But I watched her classroom enough and talked to my son to know that the children loved her. Ray stayed, because *he* was benefitting. I didn't have to like her, just her effect on my child. But know that you might have to request a change in placement or program. Ultimately, it is your child whose growth you have to advocate for.

Whatever your choice for education is, remember that every choice can be changed. Most parents end up doing an amalgam of educational placements, from private to homeschooling to public in different combinations. As your child grows, her needs change and the effectiveness of the educational placement can change. Stay on top of things, and be an active member of the team that is all working to help your child. Trust them, but be cautious.

Are We There Yet?

6

GETTING GOOD MILEAGE

Things have calmed down considerably from the chaos that was our life for so many years. We know that tantrums will end eventually; we know that some days are worse than others. We know that there are successes and there are failures. We know that our daughter is becoming who she is. We know that our son has his own unique set of challenges without the support of a label. The autism lurks around our house and most of the time it's kept at bay, only triggered by tiredness, anxiety, hunger, lack of structure, transitions . . . in other words, life.

I have, however, learned some global coping strategies for me and for our family.

Exercise

For my children, deep, stretching exercise is absolutely critical to their ability to focus and their ability to regulate their own emotional states. We call it "getting the evil jujus out." I often challenge them to a good run around the park in front of our house. They have been enrolled in formal sports activities since they were tiny because of their need for focused, large muscle, physical activity.

For me personally, yoga has been a tremendous source of strength. I find that the calm, breathing activities as well as the stretches help me center myself and, indeed, get rid of my "evil jujus." I have introduced it to the children, but it's slow going. They would rather be very active, and yoga requires concentration. However, they enjoy the stretching, so we do it in small bursts. Dion Betts (2006) has a very useful book called *Yoga for Children With Autism Spectrum Disorders: A Step-By-Step Guide for Parents and Caretakers* that we have found to be helpful.

Structure

Counting has worked so well as a coping strategy that we've used it pretty extensively. It is a dependable structure to our days. But we also have strong routines that we establish for consistency. At times, I will even ask the children how they would prefer we do things. The other day, I was fussing at Ray for not brushing his teeth—a sensory experience he does not enjoy. "What do we need to do to help you remember to brush your teeth? Would a reward work? A schedule? You can't get out of brushing your teeth—what would help you finish it?" I asked. He opted for a visual reminder and a toothbrush that lights up that he can watch while he's brushing. They crave structure, and as much as possible, I try to get them involved in the process of creating it.

I generally think through what it is that is going to happen, so that I'm very clear about consequences for their behaviors: "If you don't get in bed by the time I count to three, you will not be allowed to play quietly for 10 minutes, and I will turn the light off right now." "If you don't stop arguing over the computer game by the time I count to three, I will turn off the computer."

We've even used time as a measure to self-manage behavior. "You may have it for 10 minutes, and then it's Ray's turn." "You may play on the computer for 10 minutes and then you're done." "You have 2 minutes to put as many things away as you can. How many things do you think you can pick up?" "How long do you think it's going to take you to get dressed?" My kids love numbers, and so I use that love of numbers to help them control their lives. Of course, when they were little, I could announce how long things lasted, "Oops! 10 minutes is up!" Now, they can read clocks and I can't get away with that as easily. But it's helpful.

Targeted Rewards and Consequences

It's important to know your child and set up consequences that he wants to have happen and things that he doesn't want to occur. Know what you're going to teach your children when you're planning rewards and consequences. I learned this very clearly when my son was 3. He had colored on the walls in dramatic strokes—really expressed himself. I, of course, had my attention somewhere else. I was frustrated because I had told him *not* to draw on the walls. I informed him that when we make messes, we clean them up and that he was going to have to clean up that mess *right now*! He was thrilled! Scrubbing the walls was great fun for him. He turned a delighted smile up to me, and I realized that I was in trouble. Kids on the spectrum often love gross motor movements—actions that involve the whole arm, the whole body, things that build strength. Scrubbing the walls . . . what a great activity! I knew that we were in for many more days of colored walls if I went down this route. I informed him with great sternness that he was not going to be allowed to clean this up because we do not write on the walls and he was going to have to *sit there and watch*! I commanded him to sit on the step and watch me commence to scrubbing. He cried, and I realized that I was totally doing a Tom Sawyer. To this day, Ray has not colored on the walls again, and I sometimes offer for him to scrub walls as a reward for cleaning his room. Don't know how much longer I can get away with physical labor as a reward, but it's working for now. Ray is "allowed" to do dishes now and "allowed" to mow the lawn.

Brainwashing? You betcha! I have purposefully "allowed" the children to do things that I want them to do. They are not "allowed" to do dishes unless we have a quiet dinner. They will be "allowed" to help me clean the garage if they do not fight in the morning. It's all in how you look at it!

Consistency

Structure *only* works if you're consistent with it. It is so tempting when you're so tired to let little things slide. I have found that if I have the thought "Well, just this once . . . " I'm in for it. "Just this once" is interpreted by kids as "Well, if I push/scream/yell/stim enough, I'll eventually get my way. It worked once—it might work again." Gambling addicts are hooked because of the rush that they get when they win *finally*, after so much frustration. It is the winning every now and then that makes the brain get hooked. I'm telling you: You're in for trouble if you go the "Well, just this once" route.

That being said, there are lots of things that my husband and I are inconsistent on. Popcorn before bed—"OK, just today because we're watching the finale of *American Idol*." Cleaning their room—"I'll do it for you this one time, and then you're responsible." But for important things—homework, politeness, not hurting things—on those we remain consistent.

And there are lots of things that we've been pretty successful with because of consistency. My children do not run into traffic because of my absolute insistence on holding hands *every time* we cross the street. Even now, at age 8, Elizabeth and I touch in some way when crossing the street. The few times they tried to run ahead of me when they were toddlers, I would grab them, go back to the beginning, and try it again. There was one day we had to practice crossing the street 11 times before they realized that I was going to win that battle. Even today, they will be riding their bikes ahead of me as I walk, and they will stop at the corners because of the consistency of years of stopping for each other on street corners. It also helps that my children are slightly fearful of streets, a fear that I have encouraged. I notice every dead squirrel and express sorrow: "His poor squirrel mommy is so sad because he didn't hold her hand." I'm sure that someday my children will need therapy to explain their fear of traffic, but it's something on which I am consistent.

Clarifying

My son and I had a major altercation the other night when we were working on his homework. I had picked him up from his afterschool program, and had asked, "Do you have everything?" He confidently replied, "Yup!" When we got home, he was missing his homework calendar. I was fussing at him and said, "You said you had everything!"

In tears, he replied, "Mommy, I don't know what you mean by 'everything'!"

I have to constantly rephrase things, break them down into component parts. Typical parental orders like "Clean your room," "Get dressed," "Are you ready for school?" or "Do your homework" get lost in the muddle of language that surrounds Elizabeth and Ray. I try to keep my patience as I break global ideas into specific tasks.

I sometimes have to take a very analytic path as well. My two are very sensitive, and any sort of reprimand can lead to an orgy of tears or completely shutting down. Ray has what we call his "scowl," where he will go into a black, dark place where he cannot hear you nor respond to you. I have learned to ask them to tell me what worked and what did not. When they get in trouble, or don't do well, or make a mistake, I have learned to keep them in the world by asking them, "What did you do right, and what happened to make it go badly? What else could you have done?" This strategy depersonalizes the emotions that they can't handle, and uses their analysis for rules.

This has huge social implications of course. Other mothers and teachers use global commands all the time. "Be nice" is a rather global idea to get along. "Be polite," "Treat others as you would like to be treated": All of those rules for living have to be explained, broken down, and shown how they connect to other things. "That was *not nice*" is a firm statement in our house.

Crisis Mode

There are many children with high-functioning autism who, during moments of anxiety, will appear to purposefully stir things up. A friend of mine's son, who is diagnosed with high-functioning Asperger's syndrome, has been known to urinate on her curlers, smear feces, go into his brother's room to break the toys, and to generally cause mayhem. Susan Senator (2005) discussed how her son would bite, pinch, and pull the hair of people he was around. In her memoir, Helen Keller (Keller, Sullivan, & Macy, 1903) shared how she became a "wild thing," scratching and screaming at her family. Other children will thrash around, pound their head until it bleeds, or bite.

Such actions typically are done because the child needs some form of interaction, some form of stimulation, or some reassurance of ritual. It is easier to get attention and emotional responses doing negative things than it is to get positive attention. And you can almost be guaranteed a response with violent behavior—a predictable reaction that can therefore be counted on. And screams and yelling are more intense than hugs and smiles. When a child is particularly anxious or feeling disconnected, any attention can ground him. Tito Mukhopadhyay (2000) noted that he felt disconnected from his body and couldn't understand what he felt, unless it was a very strong feeling. Some descriptions have included things like "flying apart," or "disconnected," and such feelings can bring out a "fight or flight" sensation. Susan Senator (2005) related how her son would have dilated eyes and rapid breathing. Strong sensations, such as deep pressure or strong emotional reactions can be the only things that children with autism feel keep them together—emotionally and physically. They are, in a sense, fighting for their lives.

This understanding, of course, doesn't help when you or someone close to you is the one being bitten, screamed at, or otherwise abused. Although ignoring some behavior can reduce its impact, often the child will just try harder for a reaction, and when someone is being hurt, you cannot ignore such behavior.

There are, however, a variety of other choices for you. You can:

* Remain passive, even in the face of great volume. If the child is trying to provoke a response, then removing that response can eventually decrease the behavior. Consistency is key, as is depersonalizing the situation. The child does not truly have this level of anger at *you*—just at the situation in which he cannot count on a reaction.

* Remove the child from the situation, calmly and efficiently, with little to no reaction. In a school I worked at, they had "removal rooms" in which children were placed if they were behaving violently. There was no yelling back at them, no matching of emotion, just removal to a room where they could not hurt themselves or others. In our house, we use a small room that is darkened when my children are out of control. I'm usually crying on the other side of the door, holding the knob, but I'm crying quietly, and I will only repeat the expected behavior in a monotone voice.

* Many "old school" adults will encourage physical discipline at times like this. I've been told (and so many friends of mine relate that they've been told this also) that "What that child needs is a good spanking." As a parent of a child who's different, you *know* that a "good spanking" often will simply make the situation worse. Spankings moderately work as a temporary means of discouraging a child who is using a tantrum or misbehavior to get what he wants. For a child is truly out of control, an adult who also is out of control will terrify him, and it will take even longer for him to return to a state where he can hear you or respond to you. I have bittersweet memories

of Ray, 5 years old and tear-stained, desperately trying to catch his breath after a tantrum, repeating, "I be good now. I be good now" as he fought for control. He needed me to model for him, and encourage him to find his own control. He did not need me to be shrieking at him, or spanking him, or doing anything other than providing a haven from his own swirling emotions.

- Interrupt the crisis early on, before it escalates, with a strong, positive reaction. I watched a child once who had let out a good scream and was building rapidly toward a tantrum. His teacher sat down hard next to him with a dramatic movement and threw back her head and laughed—not at him, but a shout of laughter. He looked startled, and then let out a laugh along with her. She gave him a big hug and held him firmly. You could see him physically begin to calm down as the tension eased out of him. The need for stimulation is there and is great, but you can provide a dramatic response that is positive. Temple Grandin (2006b) shared in her autobiography that she would squeeze herself in small spaces when she was stressed out. She was seeking grounding feedback, and the pressure all over helped her regain her control. I have found that tickling helps my children when they are needing strong responses from me.

- Breathe, just breathe. Many parents report that talking to their child during a meltdown can exacerbate the issues. Deep breathing can (a) help *you* calm down, and (b) model for your child breathing techniques that she can use to center herself. When a child is heading into crisis mode, learning to deep breathe through it can reduce the stress cortisol levels, and according to Stephen Porges (2007), increase the blood flow to the parts of the brain that are shutting down, reducing the "fight or flight" reaction that is a crisis attack. I have found that yoga has helped me tremendously to find that core of quiet within myself through breathing. I have a very sweet memory of when I was 6 years old, being on my bed with my own mother, coloring in a coloring book with her. I was aware of her breathing, and I changed my breathing to match hers. The peace I felt as we breathed together in synchronization was so powerful that I felt part of her and part of a bigger universe at the same time. Breathe with your children and encourage them to breathe with you.

- In very severe cases, the medication risperidone, an antipsychotic medication, has been found to reduce irritability in children with autism. Recently approved for use for children with autism, although used off-label for some time, it has been found to reduce rapid changes of mood and self-injurious behaviors. It is important to try behavioral therapy both before and during the use of medication. It also is very important to stay in communication with your doctor about possible side effects, such as drowsiness and weight gain.

It is important sometimes to "Declare victory and get out," as Susan Senator (2005) said in her memoir (p. 217). Every year, month, week, and day will bring new challenges. The need for consistency, clarity, and structure does not change, but the way in which you make those happen will change, based upon the needs of your child. Be flexible, enjoy the ride, and know the incredible difference that you can make in the life of your child.

Siblings, Spouses, and Other Passengers

7

SIBLINGS

Although Elizabeth is the focus of this book because of her identified autism, there have been some significant effects on the rest of our family—especially her younger brother.

Tired . . . So Very, Very Tired

Autism, particularly high-functioning autism, is exhausting. And your level of tiredness gets worse. Being a mother of an infant is exhausting by itself. Add unrelenting crying, vague fussiness, trying to figure out *what* is causing the problem, having glimpses of skills that then disappear, trying to find the right type of therapy, researching until late in the night, not sleeping, vague worry that something's really wrong, and frustration that no one seems to know how to help you . . . and well, you're tired.

Tiredness is the demon that we fight constantly. When the children are tired, their challenges are so much worse—many more tears, sensitivities, lost words. And when I'm tired, my sense of control slips and I end up shrieking at the children. There is an interesting link between sleep disorders and autism. I don't know which comes first; it's a chicken and egg argument. Does lack of sleep exacerbate autism or does autism create sleep disorders? A 2007 study by Dr. Nicholas and colleagues from the University of Wales, found that there is a genetic interruption in the genes that regulate a child's internal clock and sense of sleep rhythms, and this appears to be related to autistic behaviors. I do know that generally I have been blessed with good sleepers. When we all sleep, we can all cope so much better. And when we don't . . . oh Lordy!

In our house, getting to sleep has become a 2-hour ritual. We have the bath, the book reading, the rocking, the last drink of water, the singing, and the white noise machine. My son has me kiss him in a particular order. First the kiss on each cheek, then the touching of cheek to cheek with a hug. Then, two air kisses and two air hugs and then, and only then, can he settle down and go to sleep. My kids also *need* a lot of sleep. I am the "mean" mommy who hauls her kids in for bed at 8 p.m. not to get up until 7:30 a.m.

I, of course, am exhausted myself after this ordeal, and generally pass out soon afterward. I'm lucky if I get to laundry. My husband and I joke that our son was born as a result of my total exhaustion. Elizabeth was 6 months old, fussy, and I was totally sleep-deprived. September 11th happened, and well, I forgot those little pills for a week . . . and we have Raymond now. We laugh that it's a good thing Ray came when he did—knowledge of autism would have scared us away from having other children. Jenny McCarthy (2006) said, "Autism kicked my ass" and will not consider the possibility of another child. I have to agree with her. But Ray knew that we needed him.

Do We Have Another Child?

For parents for whom birth control is an option, there is concern about having another child once they have one with autism. It is important to know that you do have a statistically slightly higher chance of having another child with autism if you already have one. And if there is more than one child with autism in a household with autism, they often are very different from each other. However, many parents feel that their family is not complete and they want their child with autism to have a sibling so, hopefully, they can be family support for each other for the rest of their lives. The best advice generally is to be prepared for your next child to have issues, and also to be prepared for different sibling issues than are typical. But if you are prepared to love another child, no matter what, and are prepared for the challenges of raising two, then you should not be afraid. Plus, you already have an idea of the landscape of autism. But you should *not* think of having another child as a chance to get the child you "should" have gotten.

Introductions and Comparisons

We were lucky: Elizabeth welcomed Ray with open arms. She was *thrilled* to have another little person in the house. Not all children with autism are like this. A new infant and mom's catatonic state are significant changes in routine. Perhaps it was because she was so little when he was born that she didn't really remember life without him. But whatever the reason, my two are remarkably close and have always found a sense of stability and peace with each other. Do they fight and push each other's buttons? Of course. But they have been remarkably "there" for each other and understand each other at a very deep level. We call them the "Irish twins" because they are so much alike, so close in age, and well, my husband's father was Irish.

Other families are not as lucky. Many children with high-functioning autism will reject the new baby, and many typical siblings will not understand their sibling who has autism.

Child With Autism as the Older Sibling

If your child with autism is older, you should carefully prepare him for the change in schedule when the new baby comes home.

Be prepared for regression. *All* children will regress when a new baby comes into the picture, and a child with autism will feel the change in schedule in an extraordinarily strong manner. Regression for a child with autism can be pretty dramatic, and it might mean going back to the diapers you just grew out of or increased thumb sucking or a greater pulling away from the environment, wanting you to come and pull him or her back into the world.

You can talk to him about the baby and bring in a baby doll to model behavior. Do not be surprised if your child with autism does not necessarily recognize the new baby as something other than a really noisy doll. I knew a family whose son with autism tried to put his baby sister in the garbage can because he wanted to get rid of the doll.

If you have pets, you can put your child in charge of helping the animal adjust to the baby. We have found that our pets are invaluable in helping our children adjust to new settings, and Elizabeth and Ray both cling to our dog, Cody, whenever they are anxious about something. By reassuring the pet, children can sometimes work out their own issues. It's important to have the right animal, however. Ray frequently hauls around our cat Chrissie, who is amazingly tolerant of his need for snuggling. Our other cat, Nellie . . . not so much.

Books also are helpful because they provide visuals about having a baby around. Susan Senator (2005) made a crisis book for her child to view before the arrival of a sibling, but there are many already-published books on the topic such as *The Berenstain Bears' New Baby* by Stan and Jan Berenstain. You should emphasize that love is something that grows the more there is. You might grow a seedling plant for a few weeks to show your child that the longer a plant grows, the bigger it gets, just like love does. The bigger a family is, the more love there is. One more person will add to the love, not divide what is there.

If the hospital will allow it, allow the child to visit the hospital where you will give birth. Do trial runs where your caretaker stays over at your house with your child so that he is not confused when you disappear.

Stick to your old routine as much as possible when the new baby comes. You may not be as coherent as you would like, but if your child has swim class, bundle up the new baby as soon as possible and head out to the pool. I was very aware of the differences between the wonderful "cocooning" I got to do when Elizabeth was born (where we shut out the world and I got to live on her schedule), and the way that Ray had to fit himself into Elizabeth's preexisting life. Ray was breastfed in many more cars and on the run much more than Elizabeth. Such is the life of a younger sibling, with or without autism.

Child With Autism as the Younger Sibling

Your older, perhaps typical child may not understand why you are so absorbed with the issues of the new little one. It's hard enough for an older sibling to lose her place as "baby," much less when that new baby is so very demanding in terms of your time, energy, and worries.

It is impossible to give the same amount and type of attention and energy to two children—even typical children. And siblings are masters at pointing out how unfair this is. You also may be aware of the unequal distribution of time and energy you can provide your two children and feel badly about this. The best piece of advice I ever got was to remind the child that you are absolutely there to give her exactly what she *needs*, and that if it she was in the other child's situation, you would be doing the exact same thing for her as well. Do not try to make it up to the other child, but do try to focus on what it is that she might need. This might be trips away without everyone else. This might be going to her soccer games. This might mean an extra cuddle before bed. This also might be teaching her how to wash the dishes or clean her room when she is 6 so that you can be relieved of a household task. Independence is a worthwhile goal, but you need to couple it with appreciation and value for that child.

"Not Fair"

It is difficult to explain to your child who does not have autism why his or her sibling is the way he or she is. Susan Senator (2005) talked about how her youngest son asked if his brother's brain was "broken." It's a useful analogy. A friend of mine, another fan of Susan's book, was asked by her typical son why his brother was "so weird." She explained to her son without autism that everyone is different; everyone has things that don't work the way we would want them to; and then she tickled him, telling him that his feet must be broken because they were really smelly.

Some children who perceive that their families are so absorbed with the autism of their sibling may develop "problems" of their own. When they see the attention and concern of the parents over anxieties or sensitivities, they also may develop some issues in order to get some attention as well. Therapy for the family is a good idea if this occurs. Clearly, there needs to be good communication between the parent and the child that he is to help his sibling, but not feel responsible, nor try to claim disability for his own.

When I teach the concept of fairness to teachers, I use an analogy. I find two students who are very different from each other in height—one tall and one "vertically challenged." I tell the class that they have both earned a reward; they both worked hard, they both did what they needed to do to earn it. And the reward, a candy bar, is on top of the projector, or the molding around the door, or somewhere in the room that is very high. "Who has access to the reward?" I ask. Clearly, the taller person can reach it better. Is it fair to require the shorter person to reach the candy bar? Of course not. The shorter person can ask the taller person for help (peer assistance), or use a chair (special access or materials), in order to reach the same reward. Would it be "fair" to give the taller person a chair? No, because he doesn't need it. The shorter person, by reason of his biology, cannot reach the goal. It would not be "fair" to deny the shorter person a chair, and so we cannot ask people with disabilities to do things that their disability does not allow them to do. We have to provide them a way to get there, and to deny them that is truly *not fair*!

Having a sibling with a disability isn't necessarily a bad thing. Sandra Harris (1994), author of *Siblings of Children With Autism: A Guide for Families*, noted that typical siblings of children with disabilities are more responsible, more caring, and more tolerant of differences than other children. They learn early that they play a very important role in the family and often move into a caretaker role. If they are younger, they can learn self-confidence because they sometimes move beyond their older sibling. If they are older, they can learn how to be responsible and compassionate—a lesson that many children need to learn.

"Dusted" With Autism—Comparisons

Many siblings, while not exhibiting classic or severe autistic behaviors, appear to be "dusted" with autism, as Susan Senator (2005) said in her wonderful book. One of the reasons that my children get along so well is that they undoubtedly recognize in the other some of the same issues that they face. I can't help it: I was always watching my younger child like a hawk for symptoms of autism. And boy, did we find them, but not enough for a label. Psychologists agree that he's on the spectrum, and he has his own host of challenges, but nothing clear-cut enough for a label. And that label provides services.

When he was born, Elizabeth was 15 months old, and I was so lost in a fog of infant/toddler issues that I didn't have time to observe either of them for a while. I now know that I was probably battling postpartum depression, but I was too tired to deal with it. Between the screaming of two children and trying to keep them both clean and fed, I lost a few months there. I did make it to Elizabeth's pediatrician's visits, and tried to go back to work part-time because we needed the money.

When Ray started babbling right on cue at 14 months, I wanted to celebrate. When he didn't start walking until 13 months I worried until I read that he was right on track. I relaxed. I hauled him around to all of

Elizabeth's speech therapy sessions and all of her occupational therapy sessions. I put him into the same Montessori school she was in. He started to talk, and she started to talk to him. Life was good.

I was thinking that God had given me another child to help me with the first one, until Ray started showing strange symptoms of his own. Ray gained not an ounce between age 1 and age 2. Not one. In a most apologetic manner, the pediatrician noted that she had to make a report to Social Services because he was showing signs of "failure to thrive" and they had to make sure that we were not at fault. I couldn't help but wonder: If we were poor and from a different culture, would we have gotten the same apologetic tone? It was not the first and certainly not the last time I saw that we were treated differently because of our educational background.

I was sick with worry. From the beginning, Ray was a fussy eater. He seemed to have terrible gas pains, intestinal cramping, and kicked constantly. I now know that gastrointestinal issues are a symptom of autism, too. But I didn't know then. Elizabeth had bouts of fussy eating, but nothing significant. We could generally find a substitute. I nursed both of my children but Elizabeth had weaned herself when I got pregnant with Ray when she was 6 months old, and had quickly and easily moved to baby food and drinking formula from a sippy cup. Ray, on the other hand, was another story. He would eat enough to not be hungry any more, as opposed to eating until he was full. Then, less than an hour later, he would be screaming with hunger again. I would have to squirt the milk into his mouth to get him to latch on. He would act very surprised and nurse hungrily for a few minutes until the hunger pangs were gone. Both of the children were lactose-intolerant, and I cut out much of my regular food from my diet to nurse them. I was constantly feeding him. He also refused to take a bottle. I left him with his father once when I had to be gone all day conducting a workshop. I left a whole refrigerator of breast milk and a bottle. When I returned, I had a very pale husband, a weak and gasping infant who had not eaten in 8 hours, and a daughter who let out a roar of anger when she saw me. From then on, I took Ray with me everywhere. He and I went to workshops I was leading, a conference in Iowa, and to meetings with school administrators. It wasn't that I was that committed to breastfeeding, but my son was.

When he turned 2, which happened to coincide at the same time my daughter was fully involved with speech and occupational therapy, he was tested for everything gastric. He was tested for Crohn's disease, celiac disease, some form of allergies, and diabetes. On one particularly hellish day, I took him to the doctor's office in the morning where they injected him with something (I was so overwhelmed at that point that I was losing track of what was being done to whom), then he had to wait an hour and get hot, and then go back and have his sweat tested. We lived in Florida, so I dug out his snowsuit we used when we visited the grandmothers in colder climates and had him play on the playground for an hour. He cried and fussed and tried to take it off. I fought with him and tried to keep my daughter occupied as well. She was happily playing on the playground and didn't want to go walking around the complex. Ray wanted to go for a walk and wanted nothing to do with the playground. I figured that in fighting with me, he was at least working up a sweat. We then went back to the doctor's where they had to tie him down to test his sweat and get blood drawn. Then, we all had to go and take Elizabeth to speech therapy, and then I left to go and teach an evening class. I cried—*a lot*—that night.

The tests all came back negative, of course. I remember the doctor looking at him and saying, "Look little man. Either you eat, or you'll be put into the hospital where you'll be tied down and have tubes put into your arms to make you eat." Ray gained 2 ounces over the next 2 weeks and still hates doctors. For his 5-year check up, he hid under the table and I had to drag him out and hold him while the doctor took his vitals. She remarked dryly that his lungs were working just fine.

But Ray has always been a great talker and can carry on a conversation for hours on end with people he knows. However, he does not have great eye contact with people he does not know and will respond to "How are you?" from strangers with grunts or will hide behind a parent. He loves getting dirty and playing with water. He's quite popular with his friends at school. But he has always cried when I sing (and I don't sing *that* badly!) and hates it when I read him a story with an accent. He *hates* wearing shoes. When he's tired, he puts his hands over his ears and is comforted by petting our cats. On the spectrum—oh yes. But not enough for a diagnosis.

Interactions

My two are still little, so there's more to come, but I can certainly see how autism has impacted the interactions between them. They tend to share friends and this can lead to some clashes.

Although my two haven't done this, other friends of mine tell me of times that their child without autism sets off the other on purpose. All children will push each other's buttons on purpose just to aggravate the other one. My friend Rachel has a story that describes this process of how sibling rivalry can use the characteristics of autism to "get" to each other:

> We were riding in the car and there was this discussion going on in the backseat about dinosaurs. They were 3 and 4 at the time, and the conversation was similar to what you would expect for their age: basic dinosaur facts. Then the discussion started to heat up when it came to color. I am not even sure how it escalated, but Ben, my son with Asperger's syndrome, was telling Robert that dinosaurs were green, which is apparently true for many, but Robert kept saying that they were white. Now Robert is a really smart kid, and even at 3, he knew what color most dinosaurs were and knew white was not the right answer, but he also knew that it would get Ben going. Back and forth they went . . .
>
> Ben: "Green. Dinosaurs are green."
> Robert: "White . . . they're white."
> Ben: "Green!"
> Robert: "White."

Ben: "GREEN!

Robert: (pause) "White."

I finally had to intervene. "Stop it, just stop it, the two of you!"

Then as things calmed down and all was quiet, this tiny voice whispered, "Dinosaurs are white."

"MOM!!!!!!!!! Robert says dinosaurs are white! MOMMMM!!!"
The tears started flowing and the rage was full blown.

There are a number of support groups for siblings of children with autism, both online and through advocacy associations. I have listed many of them in the Appendix, which covers information on advocacy and activism and provides a list of resources to help you. I also would recommend therapy when or if a sibling appears to having a hard time dealing with his or her brother's or sister's issues. As children grow up, their needs change, so the happy little brother who went along with watching Disney videos might get frustrated at the child with autism's tantrums when he is older, or might express significant anger at some of the damage that the child with autism can inflict. If this happens, I highly recommend family therapy. Behaviors change and so do family dynamics.

SPOUSES

Let's be honest here: The person reading this book is probably a mother. If you're not, my deepest apologies, but most of the time the person doing the research, running kids around from place to place, and taking care of the day-to-day stuff is the mom. Every now and then a dad will be the "carrying parent" (the one who takes the responsibility of the "work" of having a child with autism), but it's rare. Sadly enough, there appears to be a *tremendous* rate of divorce among parents with a child with autism. The general number cited on multiple websites is 80%–85%, but there appear to be no solid statistics on this. However, it is undeniable that autism places tremendous stress upon a marriage. For marriages that are strong and parents who are willing to "grow up" and do what's necessary, there is a good chance of survival. In fact, the National Autism Association (NAA, 2009) started the first national program to combat divorce rates in the autism community in 2007. For marriages that are challenged in the first place, autism may be the very wedge that serves to drive couples apart.

When a child is diagnosed with autism, or any disability, both parents grieve the loss of their "perfect" child. Men often try to be the "strong one" for their wife and family, being what Susan Senator (2005) called the "Daddy-knight on the white stallion." Mothers can either overrely on their husband to listen, or can become so invested in the search for help that they stop listening or sharing with their spouse. Successful collaborations happen when both parents begin working together to solve the various problems that come up, rather than one solving and one reassuring. If you can form an "us vs. this thing" mentality, there's great hope of a successful parenting experience. Susan Senator spent a good amount of time in her book discussing how she and her husband worked together, had what they called a "Sweetie Treaty" (which essentially was an agreement "not to feel bad about feeling bad"), and helped each other focus on making one small change, rather than trying to fix all of the things that were going wrong.

My husband, James, was very encouraging and patient throughout this ordeal. James became very aware of personal challenges given his own family's dealings with aging relatives and cousins facing developmental challenges. In fact, one second cousin of his, Christos, had been born with a subgaleal hematoma; this occurs when blood accumulates just under the scalp during a vacuum extraction. It resulted in long-term growth trauma that impacted his speech and hearing. Having grown up alongside Christos resulted in James' becoming more enabling and understanding of personal challenge from a very early age.

James is very spiritual and that sense of self and family kept him very grounded and anchored in how he engaged with me and with the children. According to my husband, a deeper truth helps us weather the currents of emotion that pass through us during very personal challenges, like a child being diagnosed with autism. Maintaining a healthy resolve and taking a positive stance on everything that may appear insurmountable makes the journey more tolerable and keeps things more focused and directed. His positive outlook tended to bring my anxieties back to reality, or at least helped me see things in a different light.

But not everyone has a companion who can balance out their needs. Divorce can have tremendous impacts on any child, and can have very significant, but different impacts on a child with autism. The biggest stressor for the child will be both the removal of the person and the change in the routine. If the other parent was very loving, that will be a significant change. But even if the other parent was abusive, the structure and routine of that cycle will be difficult for the child with autism to release. In addition, the tension that can be found within a relationship that is deteriorating can be felt very acutely by a child with autism who may shut it, and the rest of the world, out, or act out. If divorce is something that cannot be avoided, you should seek therapy for you and for your child. The various autism support networks have significant resources available for parents who are divorcing. The presence of disability also can impact the divorce process and child support issues. Check with your state and your lawyer for specifics.

I know that my own marriage suffered greatly—we didn't even understand the depths of our challenges until years after Elizabeth's diagnosis. So much was put on the back burner that wasn't dealt with. We were in crisis mode for years and years dealing with the challenge of two children with issues, lack of family nearby, and financial stress. However, James and I problem-solved everything tremendously well. I did the research; he listened to me and gave me advice. I paid the bills; he worked full-time. I ran the children from doctor to doctor, and he kept track of them on his calendar. We are both only children, so we turned to each other every night to cry and plan the next step.

Throughout it all, he was strong and steady and focused on Elizabeth and Ray's needs—to the point that so many of our own were neglected. He, and I, let him be the strong one for so long that he didn't feel he had anyone to talk to or to share his days' events. When we got away for the first time together a few years ago, we had no idea what to say to each other that didn't involve the children.

Trying to take care of each other was very difficult. I gained weight from lack of exercise and eating too much. Ice cream really helps calm that panicky feeling in your stomach when you don't know what is coming up. I consumed pint after pint of ice cream. He found solace in work—completely absorbed by various problems and projects. Both of us suffered in our friendships because we were unable to make commitments to meet friends and we felt that we were boring our friends with our stresses. Heck, we were boring ourselves.

And oh, the financial stress—that in itself seriously strained our marriage. We borrowed *lots* of money and then even more money from my mother. She helped pay for therapy, for new clothes, for doctors' bills, for electricity, for private school. I couldn't work full time for several years and was constantly trying to juggle consulting and various adjunct teaching jobs at several universities. I would have to go to conferences to make the connections to get more consulting gigs, but the conferences themselves would be expensive. I was heartbroken the day in July 2004 when we closed the sale on our first, and last, house we ever owned. It was a lovely house with a pool in Florida that we had purchased right before Ray was born and months before all hell broke loose in trying to juggle everything. We had our fantasy house for 2 years and ended up losing it. Yet another dream lost to the shrapnel of autism.

James also was changing jobs. The growing challenges on the home-front made things that much more stressful at work. The job changes necessitated several moves for our family as well. In her 8 years of life,

Elizabeth has lived in five states. Moving and packing is a skill that I wish we didn't have. For a child who craves stability, our constant moving has taken a toll on her. And the guilt of that eats at me.

Therapy helps tremendously. For years, there was no therapy—no money, no time, and no energy for one more thing. Now that things have settled down considerably, therapy is helping us remember who we are when we're not in crisis mode—a place we haven't seen in more than 10 years. If you have no time, no energy for therapy, and are married to a stranger, my best advice for both of you is to wait it out. I had a policy of waiting 6 months to see if things got better. If at the end of 6 months, things were not better, I could think of doing something. For a girlfriend of mine, things were not better, and so she made changes. But at the end of 6 months, they always were better for us.

There *will* be a time when there is a "normal" to your days and you can deal with things. James and I stayed married given our deep love for one another and innate sense of family, not "for the sake of the children" as in the martyr-laden old days, but the realization that our anchored love and the family unit are for us at the core of our beings. We were both willing to get past the hurt we had done to each other, the years of anxiety and stress, and remember why we were together in the first place. Besides, I *really* like him! And he is such a great dad and man . . . I couldn't lose that.

ANGELS

Recently, Tina, a friend of mine, was wondering what were the factors that "cured" her son Brandon, who no longer qualified for services through the school system. She knew that he had made tremendous strides, and even marveled that of her three children, he was now the easiest one to understand and manage! She credited her actions and some of her ex-husband's, but she noted that "Jen" had made some of the most significant impacts on her son's development. "Who is Jen?" I asked. Jen was the teenage nanny who helped her for several years, and took great pride and enjoyment out of working with Brandon. "Jen was our angel," Tina said fervently.

You will find the right people at just the right times in your life. They will pass through your life, and you may have to eventually say goodbye to them, but they will leave tremendous growth behind them. Although you can't guarantee an angel, you can appreciate all of those who come into your life to help you.

We asked a lot of our angels. They had to handle tantrums, sibling fights, fussy eaters, stimming behaviors, *and* come up with ideas to help the children manage themselves and track the changes. We came up with the idea of crisis books from Irene, who wrote cute little books for the children about major events that were coming up. We learned to sneak vegetables into Ray's muffins from Emmy. We had an opportunity to teach the children the effects of their behavior one day when Elizabeth was being particularly awful to Miss Lori, who seriously thought about leaving us as our babysitter. We all had a long talk about how actions have consequences and friends can love you, but not want to be around you if you do not treat them nicely. Miss Nicki would take them to Six Flags for stimulating activity when I was too overwhelmed to face a roller coaster. (OK, maybe that wasn't asking too much of her on that one, but it was more than I could do.)

Advertising works. We found four of our nannies, including Irene, our first nanny and first angel, by running an ad at the local university. I had to be very careful that I did not hire students who I would have in class because that would create an ethical issue, and I didn't want to be grading someone who was helping me. So, I never used students from the education programs at my own university. However, I can recommend future teachers as a source for nannies. You can go to the university's career placement office, or their newspaper's classified section, and often they will run an ad for childcare for free.

Our angels have tended to be young, and on the way to a great profession. They care about children, are flexible in their work schedules and demands, and are willing to communicate with us and celebrate our child's growth almost as much as we did. They became part of our family for a year or two until their lives took them somewhere else. In each case, it was very hard to explain to my little tender souls why they had to leave. Our children still love them and talk about them. Irene (Nanny Vene), Miss Molly, Emmy, Miss Lori, Miss Nicki, Miss Amberly, and Zach have all enriched our lives tremendously.

THE REAL DRIVERS

It is important to note that, even with all of the help of our angels, my help, my husband's help, the school's help . . . the most important people in this process have been Elizabeth and Ray. It takes great courage in the face of what appears to be overwhelming fear and anxiety to keep going. I have tremendous respect for them when I see one of them take a deep breath and step into something that must be terrifying. I remember when they first moved to our current house and they were anxious about going outside to the playground right outside. Boxes were everywhere, the smells were new, the humidity was new, and there was a group of children already playing there. To get their bikes and join a new group of children who had routines and social rules that they didn't know was terrifying for them. And they did it: They rode around and around and gradually joined the pick-up game of soccer that was going on. Elizabeth came in after about an hour and hid in her closet to regroup. I knew exactly how she felt, and after a while joined her in there. It was a lovely moment of calm in an otherwise chaotic time.

I also appreciate their ability to forgive me. I have screamed at them, I have been irritable, and I have been deeply angry at them. On one memorable day when things were just so stressful that I was snappy and hot, Elizabeth got in my face and used a line from the Disney movie *The Game Plan* where the little girl asks her father, "Is that why you never smile?" We all laughed, my bad mood vanished, and we got popcorn to go and watch a favorite movie. I thank God that I have my children and that they are the people that they are. Autism is a map for us, and we live with it, deny its power, and work on all of us becoming the best people that we can be. And even though we all have a ways to go, it's good to know that we're all in the process together.

GIFTS FROM AUTISM

Even though most of the time, we are working against the negative effects of autism, I am reminded every now and then of its gifts. When we were recently unpacking, I was getting frustrated because I couldn't find the forks. Why I had separated the forks from the spoons and knives in the boxes was beyond me. I was banging around, trying to remember what I could have done with them. Elizabeth came in, and very calmly said, "Here they are, Mommy," as she pulled out the forks buried in the inner recesses of a box that had been opened but not unpacked. How she could see the forks and remember where they were was an ability I was in awe of. There are gifts that autism brings to not only to Elizabeth and Ray, but us, their family.

Ability to Focus

So many careers require an ability to focus in the midst of chaos. With today's rapidly changing technology, people have to learn to sift through reams of information to synthesize new ideas. Both Elizabeth and Ray have intense, long periods where they can focus. If the topic or task is interesting to them, they will maintain fixed attention spans. Of course, if the topic is not of interest to them, their attention span is like a butterfly, lightly landing, only to flit off again. However, I know that whatever they find to do with their lives, they will be able to give it the attention it needs in order for them to succeed. They do not play the "game" of social engagement well, but neither are they distracted by social activity.

Superb Memory for Events and Details

While writing this book, I could not remember the line from the Disney movie I just discussed, and so I called my children over to ask them. "Is that why you never smile?" said my daughter, craning her face to look in mine, reenacting the scene in the movie. They have phenomenal memories for events, lines, and random pieces of information. Because multiplication tables are tough and vocabulary homework is difficult, my daughter seems to think that she has a memory problem, but I am always amazed at the level of detail that she can use to describe a past event. For a very long time when he was a toddler, my son insisted that he could remember being born and he would relate small, unusual details. I wasn't quite sure what to make of that, but I had to believe him when his memory for other events was so strong.

Unique Perspective

Because they watch human behavior with such focus, my children tend to have phenomenal insight into people. They know when someone is trustworthy, when someone is lying, and when someone is pretending to be happy. They don't always know how to engage with other people, but they have a remarkable sensitivity to others' needs and moods. Ray, in particular, is our little barometer and reflects the tensions and joys around him.

I know that most of the very successful people in life were the ones who saw a new or unusual way of doing things. They aren't always the most content, but they are driven by an innate need to know or to find out.

Precision

When Ray starts something, he has to finish it. When Elizabeth is working on an activity, she has to get it just right. Such a drive for perfection can lead to tears, but it also can lead to excellence. When precision is not reached, I want my children to look at their actions in the big picture and to understand why things can't be just so right *now*. And when precision is reached, I want them to celebrate the feeling of accomplishment. Such skills are noted in many aspects of life and although I want my children to have a sense of forgiveness, I do want them to keep trying to improve things around them.

Passion

What my children feel, they feel intensely. When Ray is hugging me good night, he holds on so tight that I *know* that I am loved. When Elizabeth is removed from the activities around her, I know that she is processing it in order to deal with it. Although great emotions can overwhelm, they also can inspire. I want them to feel the warmth of the flame of passion without being burned.

Because my background also is in gifted education, I recognize many of the crossovers of their abilities. What is a strength to one person can appear as a disability to another. Oftentimes, it is only a difference, and we choose to celebrate them rather than fight them. Our quote we use sometimes is "If you can't fight 'em, join 'em!" Some things that autism has given her are just essential parts of Elizabeth and we just have to marvel at her.

Natalie Merchant has a song that captures the mixture or autism and Elizabeth, called "Wonder." The lyrics, in part, say:

Doctors have come from distant cities
Just to see me . . .
I'm a challenge to your balance
I'm over your heads
How I confound you and astound you
To know I must be one of the wonders
Of god's own creation

And as far as you can see you can offer me
No explanation

O, I believe
Fate smiled and destiny
Laughed as she came to my cradle
Know this child will be able
Laughed as she came to my mother
Know this child will not suffer
Laughed as my body she lifted
Know this child will be gifted
With love, with patience
And with faith
She'll make her way

Indeed, Elizabeth and Ray will make their way. I hope that this map
helps you in your journey also.

Appendix:
Travel Agents

Whether you join a support group, volunteer for an activist group, raise money, or simply talk to anyone who asks, there are a tremendous number of things that you can do. It is important to become a member of an organization that supports autism, if only for the power of numbers. The more members that an organization has, the more power they have to create change. And there is change needed in so many areas:

- *Public Awareness*: Just the other day, an acquaintance of mine asked, "Why the puzzle piece? I see so many people with the puzzle pins for autism. What's that all about?" She knew that there was a condition called autism and has been made aware through the Puzzle Piece campaign by a collaboration of national organizations, designed to demonstrate visually how autism is such a "puzzling" disorder. The use of the puzzle piece on celebrity endorsements, racecar drivers, and even in the shape of Bachman pretzels has been noticed, increasing awareness of the disorder. Although autism has come a long way in only a few years, it still has a long way to go to becoming understood.

- *Research*: There is so much needed research in the areas of causation and treatment of autism. Many of the other areas of exceptionality have had decades of research behind them to provide a solid research base of well-established causes and cures. Autism does not have that history and is rapidly trying to catch up. With the numbers of children affected skyrocketing, there is a significant need to find some answers.

- *Dialogue*: There needs to be continued dialogue between so many disparate fields that are working on the issues of autism. Within the field of education, gifted education and special education have much to offer parents and families of children with high-functioning autism. Outside of education, there are numerous other fields that need to contribute and collaborate. Certainly, the medical community and the educational communities need to have better discussion between them. Policy makers at the Centers for Disease Control and Prevention in charge of the immunization schedules need to be in dialogue with the researchers who are examining the risk factors of babies developing autistic behaviors. Nutritionists need to be in communication with parents and others who are investigating dietary treatments. There are so many opposing viewpoints that need to be worked through in order for real knowledge and progress to move forward.

♦ *Insurance Coverage*: So many families find themselves in a terrible place where their insurance companies won't cover the costs of the very therapies that are needed to help the child grow. Speech therapy, occupational therapy, medical therapies—they all are subject to the whim of the state and the insurance plan by which you are covered. At the time of the writing of this book, only 16 states and Washington, DC, required that their state insurance carriers cover autism. Organizations are making significant efforts to force insurance agencies to pay for initial treatment costs for children that will alleviate the eventual costs of caring for adults. Prevention and immediate treatment is always cheaper than letting a problem go. Now to convince policy makers of that.

♦ *Educational Training and Coverage*: Schools across the country, and indeed the world, are overwhelmed by the sheer number of children with autism they have to serve. Teachers are simply underprepared in their educational programs about how to serve students. There is so much more knowledge needed among the very people whose job it is to serve students directly. They need help. Now.

♦ *Laws and Policies*: There are so many, many stories of discrimination against families and children with autism. Very recently, President

Obama signed a law that includes crimes against people with disabilities as a component of hate crime prosecution. We need to enforce the laws we have and create new ones that maintain the dignity and humanity of people with differences. Recognizing what is needed to help and protect our most helpless of people must be a right protected by law. In addition, policy makers need to be aware of the latest information about autism and the medical, environmental, and educational possibilities.

However, it is critical to understand activism. Effective activism is, as an old quote says, "The difference between getting someone in your corner and cornering them." Activism is not absolutism and is highly political in nature. Things get done either incredibly slowly or incredibly quickly and much of it is based on who gets involved at what time.

There is a continuum of activism that you can choose. Just by having a child diagnosed with autism, you are involved, and that involvement can then grow in many different directions.

LOCAL ACTIVISM

Local activism seeks to make small, immediate changes in the local schools, community, or businesses. It is a more personal approach and people and their families are immediately known.

- *Informally*: As a parent of a child with high-functioning autism, you will be asked, over and over again probably, to give your advice about your neighbor's child, your neighbor's sister's child, and even the person you meet in the grocery store's sister's friend's child. You will be recognized as the person who has walked through this process and your own personal experience will lend you instant credibility. I have learned that an expert is anyone in a situation who knows more than the rest of the group about a topic. I am certainly *not* an expert about autism when compared to many of the people I read or when I go to professional conferences. However, in the classes I teach for most special education teachers, the grocery store, and my extended family, I *am* the expert and it is my job to share as much as I know. There is much to learn, but there is much to share with people who need to know more.

- *Formally*: There will probably be a local organization near you that you can join. There are support groups, activist groups, fundraisers . . . the list is endless. You can choose to lead or to support. You can literally walk, or just talk to others, or organize. Just by being present, you have contributed a great deal. Because you live in the community, you have a better chance of making grassroots differences.

STATE-LEVEL ACTIVISM

State-level activism seeks to make larger, more significant changes in the state's schools and laws. It generally involves working at a local level and the connection of a local organization or community to state-level politicians. Very often, educational and insurance reforms are the goals at the state level. Such changes take a little longer to take effect, but can have powerful impacts on the children within that state.

- *Informally*: You might be asked to represent parents of children with autism and to speak to or contact your state representative. You might be asked to sign a petition or to independently write a letter or e-mail to a state lawmaker or advocacy person.
- *Formally*: There will probably be a state organization that you can join. It is not necessary that you live near the capitol, because electronic access is so easy now. There are again support groups, activist groups, fundraisers . . . the list is endless. There will probably be a specific agenda and goal that the state organization is trying to accomplish and there will be outreach to smaller communities within the state.

NATIONAL/INTERNATIONAL ACTIVISM

National-level activism seeks to make very significant changes in the nation's awareness, research findings, and treatment of autism. Rather than making changes at the immediate local level of response to autism, national efforts tend to focus on the understanding and treatment of autism, and promoting national, and even international, networking and fundraising. Such changes take a significantly longer time than local changes, but the effects can be larger and longer-lasting.

- *Informally*: You might be asked to contact your representatives to Congress or to participate in a research study. You might be asked to sign a petition or to independently write a letter or e-mail to a national lawmaker or autism advocate. You will undoubtedly use the resources of national organizations through copying or sharing information you find on their various websites. In addition, there is a growing national impact of informal networks such as blogs, Facebook, and Twitter. The electronic media connects us in ways that were unimaginable 10 and even 5 years ago. Some of the most informational blogs I have read are hosted by mothers whose names I do not truly know and whose child I have never seen. Yet, we are all mothers and I can communicate, learn, and share with them. I also learn tremendously from people in institutions, people around the world, and people who are fighting for the rights of those with autism. There are tremendous global connections possible.

- *Formally*: There are a number of national organizations with very specific missions; many have local or state chapters. You can become a member to receive newsletters and other information but the most valuable aspect of your membership is in the support you are giving them to achieve their goals. If you believe in them, support them. There are so many mothers and families who are starting a journey; the more they can find out, the better for them. I talk to mothers of children who are teenagers going into adulthood and so many of them are dedicated to helping other mothers and families. Their passion, for not only their own children, but other children like them is truly inspiring.

Whatever your role—parent, educator, researcher, activist, family member, or person on the spectrum—each of us has a very important role to play in communicating, learning, and helping others. It's interesting that a condition that resists communication and social behaviors should require so much of it. Your little part can help tremendously.

RESOURCES

The following is a list of resources that I found helpful in my "map" for high-functioning autism. This is a partial list of everything possible, and I encourage you to seek out the many, many other resources out there. This is a map that you create as you go along, and there are lots of roads, paths, and travel agents to help you along the way.

Resources Addressing Needs of Children With Autism and Asperger's Syndrome

Asperger's Association of New England—http://www.aane.org

Autism Collaboration—http://www.autism.org

Autism Europe—http://www.autismeurope.org

Autism National Committee—http://www.autcom.org

Autism Research Institute—http://www.autism.com

Autism Society of America—http://www.autism-society.org

Autism Speaks—http://www.autismspeaks.org

Autism Treatment Center of America—http://www.autismtreatmentcenter.org

Autism Watch—http://www.autism-watch.org

Childnett.tv—http://www.childnett.tv

CHIME—http://www.chimeinstitute.org

Dan Marino Foundation—http://www.danmarinofoundation.org

EEG Spectrum International—http://www.eegspectrum.com

Families for Early Autism Treatments—http://www.feat.org

The Fathers Network—http://www.fathersnetwork.org

First Signs—http://www.firstsigns.org

The Global and Regional Asperger Syndrome Partnership—http://www.grasp.org

Indiana Resource Center for Autism—http://www.iidc.indiana.edu/index.php?pageId=32

The International Center for Reiki Training—http://www.reiki.org

International Society for Autism Research—http://www.autism-insar.org

A Little Wiggle Room—http://www.alittlewiggleroom.com

MAAP Services for Autism and Asperger Syndrome—http://www.asperger.org

National Autism Association—http://www.nationalautismassociation.org

The National Autistic Society—http://www.nas.org.uk

National Dissemination Center for Children with Disabilities—http://www.nichcy.org

National Institute of Mental Health—http://www.nimh.nih.gov

Picture Exchange Communication System—http://www.pecs.com

Sacral Occipital Therapy (S.O.T.)—http://thewaytooptimalhealth.com/Sot.htm

Stanley Greenspan (Floortime)—http://www.stanleygreenspan.com

Talk About Curing Autism—http://www.talkaboutcuringautism.org

Treatment and Education of Autistic and related Communication-handicapped Children—http://www.teacch.com

UC Davis M.I.N.D. Institute—http://www.ucdmc.ucdavis.edu/MINDInstitute

University of Louisville Systematic Treatment of Autism and Related Disorders—http://louisville.edu/childevaluation/star-autism-treatment-program

US Autism and Asperger Association—http://www.usautism.org

Wrightslaw—http://www.wrightslaw.com

National Organizations for Exceptionalities

The Arc—http://www.thearc.org

Beach Center on Disability—http://www.beachcenter.org

Centers for Disease Control and Prevention—http://www.cdc.gov/ncbddd/autism

Council for Exceptional Children—http://www.cec.sped.org

National Association for Gifted Children—http://www.nagc.org

Blogs by Mothers of and People With Autism and Asperger's Syndrome

Autism's Edges—http://autismsedges.blogspot.com

Autism Diva—http://autismdiva.blogspot.com

The Autism Hub—http://www.autism-hub.co.uk

Ballastexistenz—http://ballastexistenz.autistics.org

Day Sixty Seven—http://daysixtyseven.blogspot.com

Hopeful Parents—http://hopefulparents.org

Left Brain/Right Brain: Autism News, Science and Opinion—http://leftbrainrightbrain.co.uk

MOM-Not Otherwise Specified—http://www.momnos.blogspot.com

One Dad's Opinion—http://onedadsopinion.blogspot.com

NTs Are Weird—http://thiswayoflife.org/blog

University Students With Autism and Asperger's Syndrome—http://www.users.dircon.co.uk/~cns

IRC Chat Channels

#Asperger—http://www.inlv.demon.nl/irc.asperger

The Autism Channel—http://www.theautismchannel.com

Books by Parents of Children With Autism

Collins, P. (2005). *Not even wrong: A father's journey into the lost history of autism*. New York, NY: Bloomsbury.

In his search to understand his son's autism, Paul Collins delves into historical figures that would be considered autistic today, particularly the "Wild Boy" from the 18th century and other talented eccentrics. It describes both his family's work with his son while contrasting their process with historical perceptions.

Cutler, E. (2004). *Thorn in my pocket: Temple Grandin's mother tells the family story*. Shawnee Mission, KS: Future Horizons.

Written by the mother of one of the most prolific authors with autism, Temple Grandin, *Thorn in My Pocket* describes how she fought to keep her daughter out of an institution as a "infant schizophrenic" during the 1950s—a time where mental disorders were not understood, nor accepted in the mainstream of family life. She also traces the evolution of autism as a poorly misunderstood and frightful issue to one that is an extreme of our own humanity.

Gardner, N. (2008). *A friend like Henry: The remarkable true story of an autistic boy and the dog that unlocked his world*. Naperville, IL: Sourcebooks.

This is a very uplifting account of how a dog helped a boy with autism begin to open up and learn to communicate with others. It shows how animal therapy, often overlooked, can help treat different conditions.

Gaston, L., & Gaston, R. (2009). *Three times the love: Finding answers and hope for our triplets with autism*. New York, NY: Avery Publishers.

Describing their experiences with triplets with autism, the Gastons share their negative experiences with Applied Behavior Analysis and their search for alternative therapies. It details their battles with local schools and their choices for biomedical interventions. They have been featured on *Good Morning America* and CNN.

Grinker, R. R. (2008). *Unstrange minds: Remapping the world of autism.* **New York, NY: Basic Books.**

With a daughter diagnosed with autism, Dr. Grinker examines the worldwide explosion of autism and concludes that it is a societally defined difference that is in fact, a numbers game. He travels to, and looks at, other countries' perspectives of autism and states that the changes in numbers reflect an anthropologic shift, not a true increase. He expresses significant frustration that his daughter's strengths are ignored over her challenges.

Iverson, P. (2007). *Strange son: Two mothers, two sons, and the quest to unlock the hidden world of autism.* **New York, NY: Penguin Books.**

This is the story of Tito Mukhopadhyay and his mother who were convinced to come to the United States by Portia Iverson, the co-founder of Cure Autism Now (CAN). Together, they sought to tell their stories of how much potential their children have.

Kephardt, B. (1999). *A slant of sun: One child's courage.* **New York, NY: Harper Perennial.**

Written before autism became so prevalent, this book is one of the first to describe a parent's journey to diagnosis and treatment. It is a description of finding help, accepting differences, and developing strengths in a child who improved significantly.

McCarthy, J. (2006). *Louder than words: A mother's journey in healing autism.* **New York, NY: Plume.**

This is a great book about a mother's journey of how she found the GFCF diet to help her son. It was very warmly written and "spoke" to me because of her common sense approach.

McCarthy, J. (2008). *Mother warriors: A nation of parents healing autism against all odds.* New York, NY: Dutton.

An activist's journey, the book describes how Jenny McCarthy found a group of like-minded mothers who are working to save their children from autism through inoculation reform and diet.

Maurice, C. (1994). *Let me hear your voice: A family's triumph over autism.* New York, NY: Ballantine.

One of the first books written by a mother about rescuing her child from autism, it has served as inspiration to many mothers.

Merchent, T. (2007). *He's not autistic, but . . . How we pulled our son from the mouth of the abyss.* Noblesville, IN: Joyous Messsenger Books.

This book details a mother's search for treatments for her child's challenges that appeared to be autistic behaviors. With the help of a master herbalist and prayer, she worked to cure her son's aluminum poisoning, parasites, and yeast issues.

Notbohm, E. (2005). *Ten things every child with autism wishes you knew.* Arlington, TX: Future Horizons.

This is a great short book listing ways to understand your child with autism. From "(1) I am first and foremost a child," to "(10) Love me unconditionally," the book traces philosophical underpinnings when working with children.

Paradiz, V. (1996). *Elijah's cup: A family's journey into the community and culture of high-functioning autism and Asperger's syndrome.* Glencoe, IL: Free Press.

This book describes a mother's acceptance of her son's Asperger's syndrome and her efforts to help him develop self-advocacy skills. Rather than focusing on "fixing" him, she worked on teaching others and teaching him to develop his abilities.

Senator, S. (2005). *Making peace with autism: One family's story of struggle, discovery, and unexpected gifts.* **Boston, MA: Trumpeter.**
Senator's book about raising her 15-year-old son with autism describes the process of working with the school system, as well as information about her marital issues.

Seroussi, K. (2002). *Unraveling the mystery of autism and pervasive developmental disorder: A mother's story of research and recovery.* **New York, NY: Broadway Books.**
This excellent book is full of medical and scientific information about the GFCF diet. It traces Seroussi's path as she became a cofounder of the ANDI network devoted to dietary intervention for autism.

Stacey, P. (2003). *The boy who loved windows: Opening the heart and mind of a child threatened with autism.* **New York, NY: De Capo Press.**
This is very first book I read that gave me hope and introduced me to Floortime by Stanley Greenspan. Her son had terrible delays and improved significantly.

Whiffen, L. (2009). *A child's journey out of autism: One family's story of living in hope and finding a cure.* **Naperville, IL: Sourcebooks.**
A memoir of a mother who set up an Applied Behavior Analysis training program in her home and trained the therapists. It details her son's first 4 years as they tried multiple therapies and the consequent stresses on her marriage, finances, and livelihood.

Books by People With High-Functioning Autism and Asperger's Syndrome

Carley, M. J. (2008). *Asperger's from the inside out: A supportive and practical guide for anyone with Asperger's syndrome.* New York, NY: Perigee.

Written by the executive director of The Global and Regional Asperger Syndrome Partnership (GRASP), this is an excellent book for adults with Asperger's syndrome as it describes his diagnosis at the same time as his young son was diagnosed.

Barron, J., & Barron, S. (2002). *There's a boy in here: Emerging from the bonds of autism.* Arlington, TX: Future Horizons.

Written in collaboration with his mother, Sean Barron describes his journey "out" of the autism realm to develop his abilities. It describes his perspectives very well.

Grandin, T., & Scariano, M. M. (1996). *Emergence: Labeled autistic.* New York, NY: Warner Books.

Grandin, T., & Barron, S. (2005). *Unwritten rules of social relationships: Decoding social mysteries through the unique perspective of autism.* Arlington, TX: Future Horizons.

Grandin, T., & Duffy, K. (2006). *Developing talents: Careers for individuals with Asperger syndrome and high-functioning autism.* Shawnee Mission, KS: Autism Asperger Publishing Company.

Grandin, T., & Johnson, C. (2006). *Animals in translation: Using the mysteries of autism to decode animal behavior.* New York, NY: Harvest Books.

Grandin, T. (2006). *Thinking in pictures: My life with autism* (Expanded ed.). New York, NY: Vintage Press.

Temple Grandin has a tremendous number of books written about her experiences with autism. She is one of the foremost and most prolific authors with autism.

Jackson, L. (2002). *Freaks, geeks and Asperger syndrome: A user guide to adolescence*. London, England: Jessica Kingsley.
Written by a teenager with Asperger's syndrome, this memoir provides incredible first-person insights into the challenges faced by teens with differences.

Lawson, W. (2000). *Life behind glass: A personal account of autism spectrum disorder*. London, England: Jessica Kingsley.
Lawson, W. (2001). *Understanding and working with the spectrum of autism: An insider's view*. London, England: Jessica Kingsley.
Lawson, W. (2003). *Build your own life: A self-help guide for individuals with Asperger syndrome*. London, England: Jessica Kingsley.
Lawson, W. (2005). *Sex, sexuality and the autism spectrum*. London, England: Jessica Kingsley.
Lawson, W. (2006). *ASPoetry: Illustrated poems from an Aspie life*. London, England: Jessica Kingsley.
Wendy Lawson, less well-known than Temple Grandin, but prolific in her own right, provides excellent, clear advice on having autism.

Mukhopadhyay, T. R. (2000). *The mind tree: A miraculous child breaks the silence of autism*. New York, NY: Riverhead Books.
Mukhopadhyay, T. R. (2008). *How can I talk if my lips don't move? Inside my autistic mind*. New York, NY: Arcade.
A series of poems and stories written when he was 8, 11, and an adult, these books share Mukhopadhyay's perceptions of the efforts his mother went through to get him services and help.

Page, T. (2009). *Parallel play: Growing up with undiagnosed Asperger's*. New York, NY: Doubleday.
Formerly a classical music critic for *The Washington Post*, Tim Page recounts how he grew up smart, but socially outside of his peers. Diagnosed at age 45 with Asperger's syndrome, Tim describes how his diag-

nosis explained so much of his fascination with music, but his struggles with people.

Robison, J. E. (2007). *Look me in the eye: My life with Asperger's.* **New York, NY: Crown.**

The brother of Augusten Burroughs, who wrote *Running With Scissors*, John Elder Robison details the combination of ASD and mental illness that surrounded him as he was growing up.

Stillman, W. (2008). *The soul of autism: Looking beyond labels to unveil spiritual secrets of the heart savants.* **New York, NY: Career Press.**

Stillman, W. (2009). *Demystifying the autistic experience: A humanistic introduction for parents, caregivers and educators.* **London, England: Jessica Kingsley.**

Providing a view of what autism is like and the reasons behind many behaviors that are misunderstood, these books offer a very "human" view, as well as a deep insight into spiritualism from someone who has autism.

Tammet, D. (2007). *Born on a blue day: Inside the extraordinary mind of an autistic savant.* **New York, NY: Free Press.**

Exploring synesthesia and autism, the book details the amazing and insightful talents of a man with autism and giftedness in math and numbers.

Willey, L. H. (1999). *Pretending to be normal: Living with Asperger's syndrome.* **London, England: Jessica Kingsley.**

Written by a woman with Asperger's syndrome, this story recounts how she grew up knowing that she was smart but quirky and her eventual marriage to a sympathetic partner. The story also describes how she relates to her daughter, who was diagnosed with Asperger's syndrome early in life. The book is interesting because it's one of the few about women with this issue.

References

American Psychiatric Association. (2000). *Diagnostic and statistical manual of mental disorders* (4th ed., Text Rev.). Washington, DC: Author.

Asperger, H. (1944). Die 'Autistischen Psychopathen' im Kindesalter. *Archiv fur Psychiatrie und Nervenkrankheiten, 117,* 76–136.

Auld, M. C., & Grootendorst, P. (2004). An empirical analysis of milk addiction. *Journal of Health Economics, 23,* 1117–1133.

Autism Society. (2009). *Encyclopedia—Mental retardation.* Retrieved from http://autisticsociety.org/Encyclopedia/op=list_content/eid=20.html

Ayres, A. J. (1979). *Sensory integration and the child.* Los Angeles, CA: Western Psychological Services.

Baggs, A. (2007, January 14). In my language [Video file]. Retrieved from http://www.youtube.com/watch?v=JnylM1hI2jc

Banks v. Secretary of Department of Health and Human Services, No. 92-56084 (U.S. Court of Appeals, 9th Circ., February 3, 1994).

Barnard, J., Prior, A., & Potter, D. (2000). *Inclusion and autism: Is it working? 1,000 examples of inclusion in education and adult life from the National Autistic Society's members.* London, England: National Autistic Society.

Baron-Cohen, S., & Leslie, A. M. (1985). Does the autistic child have a "theory of mind"? *Cognition, 21,* 37–46.

Bellon, M. L., & Ogletree, B. T. (2000). Repeated storybook reading as an instructional method. *Intervention in School & Clinic, 36*(2), 75–81.

Bettleheim, B. (1962). *Dialogues with mothers.* Glencoe, IL: Free Press.

Betts, D. (2006). *Yoga for children with autism spectrum disorders: A step-by-step guide for parents and caretakers.* London, England: Jessica Kingsley.

Board of Education of the Hendrick Hudson Central School District v. Rowley (80-1002), 485 U.S. 176 (1982).

Bogdashina, O. (2002). *Prosopagnosia ("Face blindness") in autism.* Retrieved from http://www.suite101.com/article.cfm/autism_world/96900

Bombeck, E. (1983). *Motherhood: The second oldest profession.* New York, NY: McGraw-Hill.

Centers for Disease Control and Prevention. (2009). *Prevalence of autism spectrum disorders—Autism and developmental disabilities monitoring network, United States, 2006.* Retrieved from http://www.cdc.gove/mmwr/preview/mmwrhtml/ss5810a1.htm

Collins, P. (2005). *Not even wrong: A father's journey into the lost history of autism.* New York, NY: Bloomsbury.

Cutler, E. (2003). *The food allergy cure: A new solution to food cravings, obesity, depression, headaches, arthritis and fatigue.* New York, NY: Three Rivers Press.

Dabrowski, K. (1964). *Positive disintegration.* Boston, MA: Little, Brown.

Dandoy, A. C., & Goldstein, A. G. (1990). The use of cognitive appraisal to reduce stress reactions: A replication. In J. W. Neuliep (Ed.), *Handbook of replication research in the behavioral and social sciences* (pp. 275–285). Corte Madera, CA: Select Press.

Dawson, M., Soulières, I., Gernsbacher, M. A., & Mottron, M. (2007). The level and nature of autistic intelligence. *Psychological Science, 18,* 657–662.

DeJean, V. (2006). *Dyspraxia in children with autism and PDD.* Retrieved from http://67.80.203.99:98/spectrumcommunicationcenter.com/aut5.html.

Emory Autism Center. (2009). *Frequently asked questions concerning autism.* Retrieved from http://www.psychiatry.emory.edu/PROGRAMS/autism/autismFAQs.html

Erman, H. (2006). *Thoughts on choosing a psychologist for therapy.* Retrieved from http://www.selectingatherapist.com

Fein, D., Barton, M., Eigsti, I. M., Naigles, L., Rosenthal, M., Tyson, K., . . . & Helt, M. (2009, May). *Cognitive and behavioral profiles of children who recover from autism.* Paper presented at the meeting of the International Society for Autism Research, Chicago, IL.

Fighting Autism. (n.d.). *Autism—Statistics, incidence, prevalence.* Retrieved from http://www.fightingautism.org/idea

Findling, R., Maxwell, K., Scotese-Wojtila, L., Huang, J., Yamashita, T., & Wiznitzer, M. (1997). High-dose pyridoxine and magnesium administration in children with autistic disorder: An absence of salutary effects in a double-blind, placebo-controlled study. *Journal of Autism and Developmental Disorders, 27,* 467–478.

Fitzgerald, W. F. (1995). Is mercury increasing in the atmosphere? The need for an atmospheric mercury network (AMNET). *Water, Air and Soil Pollution, 80,* 245–254.

Fombonne, E. (2002). Prevalence of childhood disintegrative disorder. *Autism: The International Journal of Research and Practice, 6,* 149–157.

Forman, V. (2007). *The mother at the swings.* Retrieved from http://www.literarymama.com/columns/specialneedsmama/archives/2006/12/the_mother_at_t.html

Fossett, B. (2002). *Visual support strategies for literacy development.* Retrieved from http://www.internationalsped.com/magazines_articles/int%271%20jnl%20of%20sped.pdf

Glanz, J., McClure, D. L., Magid, D. J., Daley, M. F., France, E. K., Salmon, D. A., & Hambridge, S. J. (2009). Parental refusal of pertussis vaccination is associated with an increased risk of pertussis infection in children. *Pediatrics, 123,* 1446–1451.

Gorski, D. (2009). *The incredible shrinking vaccine-autism hypothesis shrinks some more.* Retrieved from http://www.sciencebasedmedicine.org/?p=393

Grandin, T. (2006a). *Animals in translation: Using the mysteries of autism to decode animal behavior.* New York, NY: Harvest Books.

Grandin, T. (2006b). *Thinking in pictures: My life with autism* (Expanded ed.). New York, NY: Vintage Press.

Gray, C. (2000). *The new social story book.* Arlington, TX: Future Horizons.

Greenspan, S., & Weider, S. (2003). *Engaging autism: Helping children relate, communicate and think with the DRI Floortime approach.* New York, NY: Perseus Books.

Happé, F. (1999). Autism: Cognitive deficit or cognitive style? *Trends in Cognitive Sciences, 3,* 216–222.

Harris, K. R., & Graham, S. (1999). Programmatic intervention research: Illustrations from the evolution of self-regulated strategy development. *Learning Disabilities Quarterly, 22*, 251–262.

Harris, S. L. (1994). *Siblings of children with autism: A guide for families.* Bethesda, MD: Woodbine House.

Harvard Medical School. (2009). *The sensitive gut: A Harvard Medical School special report.* Cambridge, MA: Harvard Medical School Press.

Huber-Kinslow, D. (2008). *Meeting the needs of gifted students with ASD.* Retrieved from http://muconf.missouri.edu/AIC2009/AutismHandouts/HuberE5.pdf

Indiana Resource Center for Autism. (2009). Retrieved from http://www.iidc.indiana.edu/index.php?pageId=32

Individuals with Disabilities Education Improvement Act, PL 108-446, 118 Stat. 2647 (2004).

Kanner, L. (1943). Autistic disturbances of affective contact. *Nervous Child, 2,* 217–250.

Karp, H. (2009). *Cracking the autism riddle: Toxic chemicals, A serious suspect in the autism outbreak.* Retrieved from http://www.huffingtonpost.com/harvey-karp/cracking-the-autism-riddl_b_221202.html

Keller, H., Sullivan, A. M., & Macy, J. A. (Eds). (1903). *The story of my life.* New York, NY: Doubleday, Page & Company.

Kern, J. K., Garver, C. R., Grannemann, B. D., Trivedy, M. H., Carmody, T., Andrews, A. A., & Mehta, J. A. (2007). Response to vestibular sensory events in autism. *Research in Autism Spectrum Disorders, 1,* 67–74.

Kingsley, E. P. (1985). Welcome to Holland. In S. Kirk, J. J. Gallagher, M. R. Coleman, & N. Anastasiow (Eds.), *Educating exceptional children* (p. 16). Florence, KY: Wadsworth Publishing.

Kogan, M. D., Blumberg, S. J., Schieve, L. A., Boyle., C. A., Perrin, J. M., Ghandour, R. M., . . . van Dyck, P. C. (2009). Prevalence of parent-reported diagnosis of autism spectrum disorder among children in the US 2007. *Pediatrics, 124*(4), 1–9.

Konstantareas, M. M., & Homatidis, S. (1987). Brief report: Ear infections in autistic and normal children. *Journal of Autism and Developmental Disorders, 17,* 585–594.

Kubler-Ross, E. (1969). *On death and dying.* New York, NY: Scribner.

Learning Disabilities Association of America. (2004). *Principles of IDEA.* Retrieved from http://www.ldanatl.org/aboutld/parents/special_ed/print_principles.asp

Lelord, G., Muh, J., Barthelemy, C., Martineau, J., Garreau, B., & Callaway, E. (1981). Effects of pyridoxine and magnesium on autistic symptoms: Initial observations. *Journal of Autism and Developmental Disorders, 11,* 219–230.

Lite, J. (2009). *Can hyperbaric oxygen therapy help autistic kids?* Retrieved from http://www.scientificamerican.com/blog/post.cfm?id=can-hyperbaric-oxygen-therapy-help-2009-03-13

Lovaas, O. I. (1987). Behavioral treatment and normal educational and intellectual functioning in young autistic children. *Journal of Consulting and Clinical Psychology, 55*(1), 3–9.

McCarthy, J. (2006). *Louder than words: A mother's journey in healing autism.* New York, NY: Plume.

Marsh, J. (2006). *Talking back to OCD: The program that helps kids and teens say "No way"—and parents say "Way to go."* New York, NY: Guilford Press.

Masterson, B. A., & Biederman, G. B. (1983). Proprioceptive versus visual control in autistic children. *Journal of Autism and Developmental Disorders, 13,* 141–152.

Maqbool, S. (2009). *67m children affected by autism.* Retrieved from http://www.thenews.com.pk/daily_detail.asp?id=170476

Mercer, D. (2008). *Mom convicted in autistic girl's death.* Retrieved from http://www.usatoday.com/news/nation/2008-01-17-3456189394_x.htm

Merchant, N. (1996). Wonder. On *Tigerlily* [CD]. New York, NY: Elektra Records.

Mize, L., & Hensler, K. (2008). *Echolalia: What it is and what it means.* Retrieved from http://teachmetotalk.com/2008/06/01/echolaliawhat-it-is-and-what-it-means

Mukhopadhyay, T. (2000). *The mind tree: A miraculous child breaks the silence of autism.* New York, NY: Riverhead Books.

National Autism Association. (2009). *First national program launched to combat divorce rates in autism community.* Retrieved from http://www.nationalautismassociation.org/press061207.php

National Children's Study. (2009). *Study overview.* Retrieved from http://www. nationalchildrensstudy.gov/about/overview/Pages/default.aspx

National Human Genome Research Institute. (2009). *What are the symptoms of autism?* Retrieved from http://www.genome.gov/25522099

National Institute of Mental Health. (2001). *Rett syndrome.* Retrieved from http://www.nichd.nih.gov/publications/pubskey.cfm?from=autism

National Institute of Mental Health. (2008). *The numbers count: Mental disorders in America.* Retrieved from http://www.nimh.nih.gov/health/publications/the-numbers-count-mental-disorders-in-america/index.shtml

Nicholas, B., Rudrashingham, V., Nash, S., Kirov, G., Owen, M. J., & Wimpory, D. C. (2007). Association of Per1 and Npas2 with autistic disorder: Support for the clock genes/social timing hypothesis. *Molecular Psychiatry, 12,* 581–592.

Notbohm, E. (2007). *The autism trail guide: Postcards from the road less traveled.* Arlington, TX: Future Horizons.

Oberman, L. M., Hubbard, E. M., McCleery, J. P., Altschuler, E. L., Ramachandran, V. S., & Pineda, J. A. (2005). EEG evidence for mirror neuron dysfunction in autism spectral disorders. *Cognitive Brain Research, 24,* 190–198.

Oldfield, A. (2006). *Interactive music therapy: A positive approach.* London, England: Jessica Kingsley.

Palumbo, P. (2009, May 17). *Au revoir autism: Can autism be cured?* Retrieved from http://mommadata.blogspot.com/2009/05/au-revior-autism-can-autism-be-cured.html

Philippot, P., & Feldman, R. S. (Eds.). (2008). *The regulation of emotion.* Mahwah, NJ: Lawrence Erlbaum.

Porges, S. (2007). The polyvagal perspective. *Biological Psychology, 74,* 116–143.

Richman, L. (1997). *Peaceful coexistence: Autism, Aspergers, hyperlexia.* Retrieved from http://www.hyperlexia.org/aha_winter9697.html

Rimland, B. (1964). *Infantile autism: The syndrome and its implication for a neural theory of behavior.* New York: Appleton-Century-Crofts.

Rimland, B., Crook, W., & Crook, C. (2001). *Tired—so tired! And the "yeast connection."* Newtown, PA: Future Health.

Rossignol, D., Rossignol, L., Smith, S., Schneider, C., Logerquist, S., Usman, A., . . . Mumper, E. (2009). Hyperbaric treatment for children with autism:

A multicenter, randomized, double-blind, controlled trial. *BMC Pediatrics, 9*, 1471–2431.

Section 504 of the Rehabilitation Act, 29 U.S.C. Section 706 et. Seq. (1973).

Senator, S. (2005). *Making peace with autism: One family's story of struggle, discovery, and unexpected gifts.* Boston, MA: Trumpeter.

Sensory Processing Disorder Foundation. (2009). *About SPD.* Retrieved from http://www.spdfoundation.net/aboutspd.html

Seroussi, K. (2002). *Unraveling the mystery of autism and pervasive developmental disorder: A mother's story of research and recovery.* New York, NY: Broadway Books.

Shattuck, P. T., Durkin, M., Maenner, M., Newschaffer, C., Mandell, D., Wiggins, L., . . . Cuniff, C. (2009) The timing of identification among children with an autism spectrum disorder: Findings from a population-based surveillance study. *Journal of the American Academy of Child and Adolescent Psychiatry, 48,* 474–483.

Shaw, W., Rimland, B., Scott, P., Seroussi, K., Lewis, L., & Semon, B. (1998). *Biological treatments for autism and PDD.* Manhattan, KS: Sunflower Press.

Simons Foundation for Autism Research. (2009). *X-chromosome searches help unravel complex genetics of autism.* Retrieved from https://sfari.org/news-and-commentary/all/-/asset_publisher/6Tog/content/x-chromosome-searches-help-unravel-complex-genetics-of-autism?redirect=%2Fnews-and-commentary%2Fall

Sinclair, J. (1993). Don't mourn for us. *Our Voice: The Newsletter of Autism Network International, 1*(3), 2–3.

Sinclair, J. (1999). *Why I dislike person-first language.* Retrieved from http://web.syr.edu/~jisincla/person_first.htm

Smith, M. (2009, May). *Did Mozart have ADHD?* Paper presented at the Congress of Humanities and Social Sciences, Ottawa, Ontario.

Smyth, J., & Arigo, D. (2009). Recent evidence supports emotion-regulation interventions for improving health in at-risk and clinical populations. *Current Opinion in Psychiatry, 22,* 205–210

Stacey, P. (2003). *The boy who loved windows: Opening the heart and mind of a child threatened with autism.* New York, NY: De Capo Press.

Stewart, R. (2000). Should we insist on eye contact with people who have autism spectrum disorders? *The Reporter, 5*(3), 7–12.

Szpir, M. (2006). Tracing the origins of autism: A spectrum of new studies. *Environmental Health Perspectives, 114*(7), A412–A418

Taira, M., Takase, M., & Sasaki, H. (2008). Sleep disorders in children with autism. *Psychiatry and Clinical Neurosciences, 52,* 182–183.

Talk About Curing Autism. (2009). *GFCFSF on a budget.* Retrieved from http:// gfcf-diet.talkaboutcuringautism.org

Tammet, D. (2006). *Born on a blue day: Inside the extraordinary mind of an autistic savant.* New York, NY: Free Press.

Tolbert, L., Haigler, T., Waits, M., & Dennis, T. (1993). Brief report: Lack of response in an autistic population to a low dose clinical trial of pyridoxine plus magnesium. *Journal of Autism Developmental Disorders, 23,* 193–199.

Tranguch, S., & Marino, M. (2008). *Sticky blood proteins yielding clues to autism-related deficits.* Retrieved from http://www.mc.vanderbilt.edu/reporter/index. html?ID=6222#

United States Department of Education. (2005). *10 facts about K–12 funding.* Retrieved from http://www.ed.gov/about/overview/fed/10facts/index.html

United States Surgeon General. (n.d.). *Autism.* Retrieved from http://www. surgeongeneral.gov/library/mentalhealth/chapter3/sec6.html#autism

University of California, Davis M.I.N.D. Institute. (n.d.). *Autism phenome project.* Retrieved from http://www.ucdmc.ucdavis.edu/mindinstitute/research/app

University of Louisville Medical School. (2009, September). New autism treatment earns EUREKA award from National Institutes of Health. *University of Louisville Medicine Magazine,* 4.

University of Louisville Systematic Treatment of Autism & Related Disorders. (2009). *Star autism treatment program.* Retrieved from http://louisville.edu/ childevaluation/star-autism-treatment-program

Walkup, J. T. (2006). *Newly diagnosed Tourette's syndrome.* Retrieved from http:// www.tsa-usa.org/news/NewlyDiagWebstream.htm

Wallis, C. (2009, November 2). A powerful identity, a vanishing diagnosis. *The New York Times,* p. D1.

Watson Institute. (2005). *Repetitive or unusual behaviors.* Retrieved from http://www.thewatsoninstitute.org/resources.jsp?pageId =0690200091781087595880940

Webb, J., Amend, E., Webb, N., Goerss, J., Beljan, P., & Olenchak, F. R. (2005). *Misdiagnosis and dual diagnoses of gifted children and adults: ADHD, bipolar, OCD, Asperger's, depression, and other disorders.* Scottsdale, AZ: Great Potential Press.

Wright, R. H., & Cummings, N. C. (Eds). (2005). *Destructive trends in mental health: The well-intentioned path to harm.* New York, NY: Routledge Publishing.

Yamamoto, R., Ariely, D., Chi, W., Langleben, D. D., & Elman, I. (2009). Gender differences in the motivational processing of babies are determined by their facial attractiveness. *PLoS One, 4*(6), e6042–e6046.

Yan, J. (2008). Learning-disability rates steady, while ADHD increases over decade. *Psychiatric News, 43*(17), 8–9.

About the Author

Claire E. Hughes-Lynch, Ph.D., has her doctoral degree from the College of William and Mary in the areas of gifted education and special education and is an associate professor of teacher education in the early childhood/special education program at the College of Coastal Georgia. As a former Visiting Fellow at Oxford University in the area of autism, she researches and publishes in the areas of educational interventions for children with autism, gifted children with disabilities, and Response to Intervention. She has lived with her husband, two children, three cats, and a dog up and down the East Coast. They currently live near the beach in Georgia, where they play happily in the sea.